kid chef

Nutty Parmesan-Kale Salad (page 121)

kid chef

The FOODIE KIDS COOKBOOK

HEALTHY RECIPES AND CULINARY SKILLS
FOR THE NEW COOK IN THE KITCHEN

Melina Hammer

Foreword by Bryant Terry

SONOMA
PRESS

Photography © 2016 Melina Hammer

ISBN: Print 978-1-943451-20-3 | eBook 978-1-943451-21-0

Printed in Canada

For kids everywhere,
May you feel empowered to bop around
the kitchen and create terrific food.

CONTENTS

....

FOREWORD

....

Flipping through *Kid Chef* brings back lots of memories of the time when my wife and I were figuring out how to get our 4-year-old daughter, Mimi, more involved in preparing food with us at home. As I am writing this, Mimi is sitting on her stool tearing rainbow chard leaves from their colorful stems into bite-size pieces. Because we started her off when she was two, this routine is very familiar. Initially, we gave her simple tasks like raking food scraps into the compost pail; washing vegetables; and picking through dried legumes, throwing away any shriveled ones. Maybe you started off doing similar things, helping out in the kitchen too.

It amazes us to see how confident and competent Mimi is becoming. As she gets older, her jobs will become more challenging: pounding spices in a mortar; zesting citrus with a microplane; separating the egg whites from the yolks; using a pan on the stove to sauté veggies. All the things you will learn here, plus so much more.

Preparing and cooking food builds independence when you're completing tasks on your own; it allows you to learn and practice basic math and science; it expands your palate; it gives you ample opportunities to be creative; and most important, cooking is super fun!

I am happy that you will have this book as a personal resource. It is so important to learn about cooking and proper nutrition when you're young so you can establish life-long habits that will decrease your risk of preventable diet-related illnesses. And guess what? With *Kid Chef,* you'll join a larger movement that embraces mindful cooking as a way to address the massive public health crisis facing Americans due to our unhealthy Western diet, filled with too much meat and too many sweets. Before you know it you will be making dishes for family and friends *and* passing on the cooking skills you've learned, inspiring others to join the movement, too.

Bryant Terry
James Beard Foundation Leadership Award-winning chef

INTRODUCTION

....

Welcome to the world of cooking! You may already have some kitchen know-how—maybe you've helped bake cookies with friends or fixed yourself a homemade snack. Or maybe you've never picked up a pan in your life. That's ok, too, because this book will teach you what you need to know to become a pro in the kitchen.

Cooking is not hard, but we all do start at the beginning. The more you practice, the better you get. Just keep that in mind, and don't get frustrated when a recipe isn't going the way you think it should, because *everyone* makes mistakes. Be patient, and ask for help when you need it.

In this book, you'll learn fundamental skills to secure your success in the kitchen, and tips to develop good cooking habits. Get ready to . . .

- Orient yourself in the kitchen and learn what to stock in your pantry as well as the must-have gadgets and tools you'll need to make great food.
- Participate in several cooking lessons to help you master the essential skills—like prep work, baking, and roasting—that go along with preparing a mouthwatering meal.
- Find a range of recipes to test out on your family and friends, from the impressive Potato-Gruyère Tart (page 93), to the easy—and totally fantastic—Chocolate-Cherry Bark (page 185), to the tasty Hearty Greens Strata (page 142) that works as a breakfast, lunch, or dinner.

As you find your own path to healthy eating, you'll discover that people will have different ideas about what that means. My idea of healthy eating is preparing foods that have little to no processed ingredients, healthy fats (those fats feed our brains!), and plenty of fresh fruits and veggies. Balanced meals like these, with the occasional indulgence of homemade sweets, make for healthy and happy living.

Are you ready to begin your journey into cooking? Put on your apron and let's get started!

culinary school

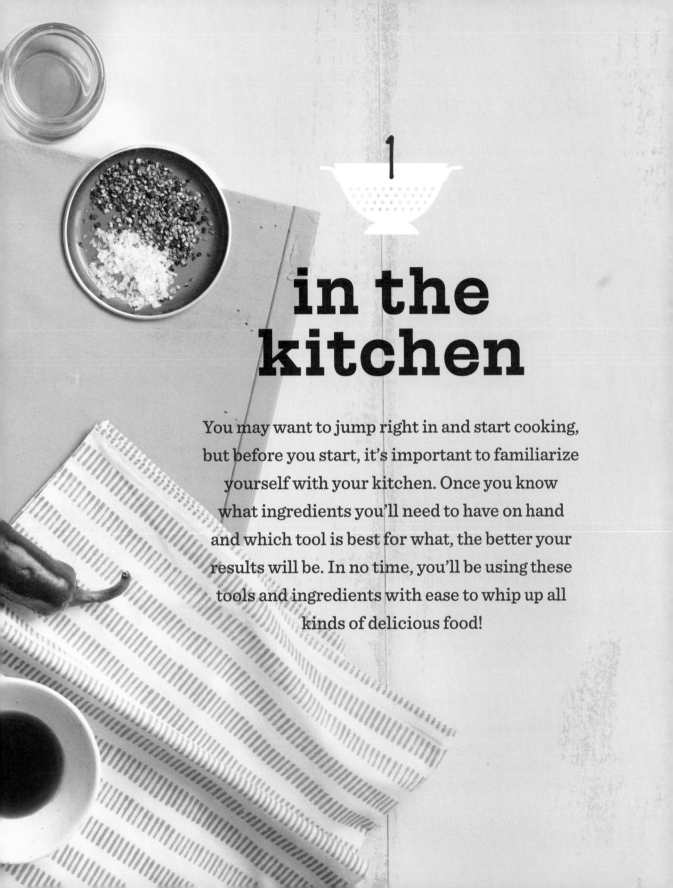

1

in the kitchen

You may want to jump right in and start cooking, but before you start, it's important to familiarize yourself with your kitchen. Once you know what ingredients you'll need to have on hand and which tool is best for what, the better your results will be. In no time, you'll be using these tools and ingredients with ease to whip up all kinds of delicious food!

BEST PRACTICES

Before you get cooking, there are a few essentials you'll need to check off to achieve good food practices in the kitchen.

1. **Make it official.** One way to make your time in the kitchen official is by putting on an apron. This helps keep your clothes free of stains and gives you an easy place to quickly wipe your hands.

2. **A clean workspace is a safe workspace.** Find a stretch of counter or table space that you can comfortably take over to prepare your recipe and clear out any nonessential items that clutter it. Then, wipe it down with a clean, damp sponge. Dry the area thoroughly before you collect your ingredients and tools.

3. **Always wash your hands.** Before working in the kitchen, always wash your hands in warm, soapy water. A high standard of personal hygiene will keep bacteria away from the food you cook and eat. Be sure to wash your hands after handling raw meat as well, since germs are often concentrated on high-protein foods.

4. **Wash your fruits and veggies.** To remove trace amounts of bacteria (from the soil or from being handled by others before you), give fruits and vegetables a gentle scrub with a soft-bristled brush (for sturdy produce like apples, carrots, and celery) and thorough rinse under cold running water (for more delicate produce like berries, lettuces, and herbs), and pat them dry with a dish towel.

5. **Handle your meat properly.** If you are preparing meat or seafood, pat it dry with paper towels before slicing or cooking. Discard the paper towels, place the meat on a plate or tray, cover, and refrigerate until ready to use.

6. **Cook your eggs safely.** Take these precautions to reduce the risk of salmonella poisoning: Do not allow uncooked eggs to sit at room temperature for more than two hours, and be sure to cook your eggs until the whites are solid.

A CLEANER CLEANER

This homemade nonchemical disinfectant works great sprayed onto counters before wiping down. In a spray bottle, mix:

- a 1:2 ratio of white vinegar to water
- a few drops of orange or lemon essential oil

Citrus fruits are natural disinfectants. Adding these enhance the antibacterial properties and make your cleaner smell nice.

TOOLS OF THE TRADE

It's not necessary to have fancy cooking equipment to get started. A few well-made basics are really all anyone needs to create a terrific dish.

There are a few kitchen tools you'll use on a day-to-day basis, such as:

- A chef's knife and cutting board
- Vegetable peeler
- Colander or strainer
- Mixing bowls
- Measuring cups and spoons

- A skillet, cast-iron preferably
- A medium-size saucepan
- Pot holder
- A heat-tolerant rubber spatula
- Wooden spoon

As you cook more recipes, you may find yourself needing more—and different—tools. Having specialty tools in your kitchen makes it possible to create more advanced dishes. Tools such as tart and springform pans, heavier metal muffin tins, ice pop molds, and appliances such as a stand mixer or immersion blender are not needed every day, but once you use them, you'll understand immediately why they exist.

As you spend time making—and returning to—recipes, you will find your favorite kitchen tools; it's kind of like making good friends over time. In the following pages, I'll cover the tools we'll use in this book.

A WORD ABOUT MICROWAVES

Professional chefs don't cook with a microwave and neither should you. Microwaves destroy the enjoyable textures and nutrients in food. They are simply a well-marketed, "convenient" replacement for other tools that do the same job. You can quickly cook and reheat foods by using a toaster oven or a saucepan, or defrost foods by using a bowl filled with cold water.

COOKWARE

 Dutch oven A heavy pot, often enameled, that works on the stove and in the oven. It's good for slow-cooking food, baking bread, and making a large batch of soup.

 Grill pan A pan with raised ridges that works like a grill on the stove top. It produces a nice char and grill marks on your food.

 Saucepan with lid A deep pan for making soups, stews, and sauces—basically, anything liquid you want to heat. Opt for a medium-size saucepan.

 Skillet A shallow pan that's versatile for sautéing, searing, caramelizing, frying, and browning. Cast iron skillets are strongly recommended as they conduct heat really well and can also go into the oven. Avoid Teflon-coated pans as they can chip over time and release chemicals like perfluorooctanoic acid (a known carcinogen), into your food.

 Steamer basket A collapsible basket used to hold vegetables and other foods over boiling water for steam cooking. It's also called a steamer insert.

BAKEWARE

 Baking dish A shallow glass, metal, or ceramic dish that can go into the oven.

 Baking sheet A metal tray, preferably rimmed, for cooking food in the oven. Used for making cookies, as well as to catch spills from overflowing juices while baking pies, lasagna, and other saucy dishes.

 Muffin pans A baking pan with built-in cups. They are available in different sizes and materials: silicone works best for easy unmolding and heavier metal tins achieve crispy edges.

 Pizza stone A ceramic, stone, or salt cooking surface. Pizza is put on the stone and placed in the oven, though sometimes the stone is heated first. It helps create a crispy crust.

Ramekins Small ceramic dishes used for baking and serving individual portions of food.

 Roasting pan Cookware used to cook meats such as whole chicken, leg of lamb, and pork. It can be used with a rack that suspends meat above the pan while catching the drippings (to make gravy or sauce) and helps air to circulate to produce crispy skin.

 Springform pan A round cake pan with a removable bottom. It's ideal for baking dishes like cheesecake and quiches, foods with delicate contents that don't allow you to invert them. It cannot be used to bake thin batters, as they will leak out of the pan's seams.

 Wire cooling rack A flat wire grid with feet that allows baked goods to rest and cool and prevents them from getting soggy with condensation.

TOOLS AND UTENSILS

 Citrus reamer A kitchen tool, often wooden, with a cone-shaped "blade" and deep troughs that extracts juice from citrus fruit.

 Colander A bowl with holes throughout used to drain pasta and canned foods and to rinse fruits and vegetables.

 Ice pop molds Containers that give shape to liquid ingredients as they freeze. Filling small paper cups or yogurt containers—or even ice cube trays—works in a pinch.

 Knives A tool with a blade attached to a handle. For different kinds of knives, see lesson 4: knife skills, page 42.

 Ladle A deep-bowled spoon with a long handle. It's ideal for transferring soup, gravy, or stews from a pot to serving bowls.

 Measuring cups Kitchen tools made of plastic, metal, or glass used to measure liquid or dry goods like flour or sugar.

Measuring spoons Small kitchen tools, often made of plastic or metal, used to measure small amounts of liquid or dry ingredients, such as spices, salt, and extracts.

 Meat thermometer A device inserted into meat to measure its internal temperature and gauge "doneness," helping you to not overcook. It's useful for cooking steaks and roasts to temperature and for safely cooking poultry and pork.

 Melon baller A utensil that produces sphere shapes from melons and other produce. It's also used to scoop seeds from vegetables, make mini scoops of cookie dough or ice cream, and shape truffles.

 Mortar and pestle A tool consisting of a bowl and a club-shaped implement used to crush seeds, spices, herbs, and vegetables.

Parchment paper Nonstick baking paper often applied to baking sheets to simplify cleanup.

 Pastry brush A utensil used to spread butter, oil, or glaze. It works well for painting egg wash or cream for a special golden crust and for glazing cakes and cookies.

 Rolling pin A long cylinder with handles used to roll and flatten dough evenly for pies, tarts, and pasta. It's also good for crushing crackers and breadcrumbs for press-in crusts and sprinkled-on toppings.

 Skewers Thin metal or wooden sticks used to hold pieces of food together especially while grilling or roasting meats or vegetables.

 Spatula A tool with a flat, flexible blade—preferably made of heat-resistant rubber, so you can scrape every last bit out of containers.

 Tongs A tool used to grip food. It's great for handling anything you're cooking with precision, whether to turn meat skewers onto the other side while grilling, or rotate carrots in a sauté pan.

Vegetable peeler A tool with a sharp metal blade used to peel the outer layer of sturdy veggies. For more stability, opt for a Y-shaped peeler.

Zester or box grater A device used to grate cheese, zest citrus, grind whole spices like nutmeg and cinnamon, and mince ginger and garlic.

Whisk A handled wire tool used to blend ingredients, smooth and eliminate lumps, and also to emulsify (combine oil and water mixtures together).

APPLIANCES

Blender or immersion blender An electric mixing device used for puréeing soups and making salad dressings, smoothies, whipped cream, and more. An immersion blender is handheld, and the blade *must* be submerged before you turn it on.

Stand mixer or handheld mixer A countertop mixer with different attachments that blends ingredients, beats dough, or whips eggs. A handheld mixer can do many of the things that a stand mixer can, but a stand mixer enables you to work hands free.

Food processor A machine similar to a blender that has a large basin to easily make salsa, pesto, hummus, dips and spreads, dough, bread and cookie crumbs for crusts, and ice cream toppings.

Toaster oven An electrical appliance that serves as a small oven. It's a workhorse for all kinds of heating tasks like toasting, melting, and caramelizing.

9 TIPS THAT WILL MAKE YOU A GOOD COOK

Commit these tips to memory, and then implement them to elevate your cooking game.

1 **Read the recipe. Read it again.** Go through the steps of the recipe mentally before gathering your ingredients and tools to start cooking.

2 **Stay organized.** A well-prepped workspace, free of clutter, is a strong foundation for success in the kitchen.

3 **Prep your ingredients.** Measure and chop your ingredients before you begin cooking, and have them at your workstation, ready to go.

4 **Clean as you cook.** No one likes to deal with a mess after producing a delicious meal. Wiping down counters, clearing your cutting board, and disposing of nonessential items as you go will make a big difference at the end!

5 **Taste, taste, taste.** Taste the food early on as you begin to cook a recipe, and taste throughout as you add ingredients. Don't wait until a dish is almost finished, because flavor is built up in layers. For dishes containing raw or undercooked meats or eggs, wait until they are fully cooked and then taste.

6 **Be patient.** A recipe doesn't always work out perfectly the first time, and that's ok. Making a less-than-perfect dish will teach you some lessons, and the next time you try it, you can apply what you learned to handle it more skillfully. You'll also get the satisfaction of knowing you stuck with it!

7 **Pay attention.** What does the food you're cooking smell like? What does it look like? How does it sound? Sometimes seconds make the difference in the success or failure of a meal. Focusing will help you save food from burning or becoming too tough or dry, and will help protect you from any cuts or burns.

8 **Use fresh ingredients.** While fresh fruits and vegetables are an important part of a delicious dish, so are fresh herbs and toasted spices: They can transform a so-so meal into one that sings with their bright, aromatic qualities.

9 **Watch others.** The more you study the people you admire and how they cook—as well as *what* they cook—the more you will absorb and the broader your own skill set will become.

STOCKING YOUR PANTRY AND REFRIGERATOR

The magic of making great food starts at the market. Choose the ripest pieces of fruit, the most deeply colored and heaviest vegetables, and the crispest, most "alive-looking" greens—even if that means sorting one piece at a time. Spend extra time choosing the best ingredients, because their flavors help make even the simplest dishes taste truly special. The following ingredients are used repeatedly in countless recipes and helpful to keep stocked in your pantry and refrigerator.

Pasta

Ridged pasta like penne is ideal for creamy, baked, or meaty sauces, while long pasta like fettuccine is great for light olive-oil- or seafood-based sauces. Lasagna noodles, tagliatelle, and other broad or ribbon-like noodles are perfect for richer, meaty sauces. As you experiment, you'll find a pasta for every sauce, and a sauce for every pasta!

- Fettuccine or spaghetti
- Macaroni
- Penne or rigatoni
- Lasagna or tagliatelle

Grains

Try to buy these bulk, because they are a better value. Stored in sealed glass jars, your beautiful array of grains is a window to inspiration and will keep from going stale.

- Barley
- Brown rice
- Quinoa

Legumes

You can buy preservative-free canned beans, but it's best to buy dry beans and soak them when you plan to use them. It's more satisfying knowing you cooked them, and you have more control of what's in your food.

- Black beans
- Cannellini or Great Northern beans
- Chickpeas

Nuts and Seeds

It's helpful to keep a wide variety of these on hand. For snacking, roasted and lightly salted is a good bet. For cooking, buy nuts and seeds shelled and raw and toast them yourself.

- Almonds
- Cashews
- Flaxseed
- Hazelnuts
- Pecans
- Sesame seeds
- Sunflower seeds
- Walnuts

Spices

Whenever possible, use whole spices. They have a longer shelf life, toast more easily—which brings out their flavor—and are more aromatic when grated.

- Bay leaves
- Cayenne
- Chili powder
- Cinnamon
- Coriander
- Cumin
- Mustard seeds
- Nutmeg
- Paprika
- Peppercorns
- Red pepper flakes
- Salt (kosher and sea salt)

Oils

Hands down, you will turn to olive oil again and again as you cook. Select the highest quality that your budget allows. Safflower or peanut oil is good for high-heat cooking such as frying. Raw coconut oil works better for lower-heat cooking and baking.

- Coconut oil, raw
- Olive oil, extra-virgin
- Safflower oil or peanut oil
- Sesame oil, toasted

Flour

You can use all-purpose flour (unbleached is best), but it's a very good idea to incorporate whole-wheat flour for its nutrients and healthful benefits. Whole-wheat flour is heavier and denser and behaves differently from all-purpose flour. In a recipe using all-purpose flour, you may substitute whole-wheat flour for one-third of the called-for amount.

- All-purpose flour
- Whole-wheat flour

Vinegars

If you have to choose between stocking up on vinegars versus oils, I recommend widening your vinegar selection first. They bring so much personality to a wide variety of dishes.

- Apple cider vinegar
- Sherry vinegar
- White vinegar
- White wine vinegar

Sweeteners

Keep honey in your pantry at all times, preferably from a local farmer. Things like confectioners' sugar are really only needed if you plan on baking.

- Brown sugar (light and dark varieties)
- Cane sugar
- Confectioners' sugar
- Honey
- Maple syrup

Dairy

Ideally, use milk, cheese, and butter from grass-fed cows. The label should read "grass fed" or "pasture-raised." The best eggs are from pasture-raised chickens and have bouncy, richly colored yolks.

- Buttermilk
- Cheddar
- Eggs
- Feta
- Gruyère
- Haloumi
- Heavy cream
- Parmesan
- Ricotta
- Whole milk

Fruits and Vegetables

As your budget allows, choose fruits and vegetables that are organic. Not only will you notice a richer flavor, you'll also avoid eating foods with pesticide residue on them.

- Carrots
- Celery
- Kale
- Lemons
- Potatoes
- Sweet potatoes
- Swiss chard

Alliums

Strong-smelling or "aromatic" vegetables such as onions, scallions, garlic, leeks, and chives are a standard in almost every recipe, creating the first layer of flavor in a dish.

- Chives
- Garlic
- Leeks
- Onions
- Scallions

Herbs

Buy fresh herbs whenever available, and comb through the bunches on display for those that have the greenest, most alive-looking shoots. They will taste better and last longer.

- Basil
- Cilantro
- Mint
- Parsley
- Rosemary
- Sage
- Thyme

2

culinary skills

This chapter serves as your cooking class. You will learn proper techniques for reading a recipe, measuring ingredients, using the stove top, cutting with a knife, preparing your ingredients, and baking and roasting in the oven. Do the lessons in order and complete the recipe tutorial with each lesson so you can practice what you've learned. Remember cooking is a skill that gets better with practice!

READING A RECIPE

Recipes are a road map to what you want to cook. But ultimately, you are the chef. Serving suggestions—and even the recipe itself—should be used as a guideline for you to adapt to your own tastes and available ingredients. Using recipes becomes even more fun as you begin to feel more confident in your personal cooking style. Then you know you can modify elements and turn out something wonderful—maybe even better than the original recipe!

Always read the entire recipe and the instructions a couple times fully to be sure you know how to perform each task and that you have all the tools and ingredients you need. I've created the **Glossary** (page 189) to provide definitions for any recipe terms that you might not understand.

Here are the parts that make up a recipe:

(A) Title This is what you are going to make. Sometimes the title also tells you about how you'll prepare the food, such as "Roasted Chicken."

(B) Time required Prep—short for preparation—includes time spent chopping, measuring, or stirring. Cook time indicates the actual time in the oven or on the stove. Freeze time is listed as well for certain recipes that need it. This helps you plan your time accordingly.

(C) Servings This is important to note, as it tells you if the recipe makes enough to feed your guests. If not, it's usually easy to double a recipe.

(D) Ingredients A list of foods you need to make the recipe, organized in the order in which they are used.

■ Some lists indicate how to prep the food before you get to the instructions (i.e., "2 tablespoons finely chopped fresh parsley").

■ Salt and pepper may not include an exact measurement. This means you will add these to your taste.

(E) Tools / Equipment These are the devices you'll need to make the recipe. However, basic equipment such as spoons, pot holders, and measuring cups will not be included in this list. Also, since you'll probably use the chef's knife most of the time, knives will only appear in the list if a different kind is required, such as a bread knife or paring knife. Sometimes you can substitute a different tool for one you don't have, for example, a thick wooden dowel instead of a rolling pin.

LESSON 1 RECIPE TUTORIAL
garlic bread

PREP TIME
5 minutes

COOK TIME
8 minutes

SERVES

4

**TOOLS /
EQUIPMENT**

Fine grater

Small bowl

Bread knife

Aluminum foil

Baking sheet

1 stick butter, at room temperature

2 garlic cloves, finely grated

2 tablespoons finely chopped fresh parsley

Freshly ground black pepper

1 baguette or ciabatta loaf

Flake salt, such as Maldon

Preheat the oven to 375°F.

Mix ingredients.
In a small bowl, mix together the butter, garlic, and parsley, and season with pepper.

Slice the baguette, and spread the butter mix.
Using a bread knife, cut the baguette on the diagonal into 2-inch segments without slicing all the way through. Use a butter knife to spread all slices, both sides, with the butter mixture, and sprinkle with salt. Cut the baguette in half, and wrap each half in aluminum foil.

Bake the garlic bread.
Lay the foil parcels on a baking sheet. Using a tea towel, remove one parcel after 5 minutes and give it a gentle squeeze. If it is warm to the touch and feels firm from developing a crust, then it is ready. If the bread is still soft and has more give, put the parcel back in the oven for 2 to 3 more minutes.

Serve.
Open the foil parcels and allow to cool for a few minutes. Serve warm alongside a hearty dish of pasta, like Pasta with Homemade Tomato Sauce (page 134).

TRY INSTEAD For extra-crispy garlic bread, after 5 minutes of baking, open the foil to expose the bread and turn the oven to broil. Broil for 1 to 2 minutes, until the garlic bread becomes deeply golden brown.

YOUR GROCERY BAG

When it comes to shopping, the best approach is to make a weekly plan of what you're going to cook, consult your recipes, and create a detailed shopping list.

- **Make a list.** Jot down all the ingredients you don't already have in your refrigerator or pantry. Make your shopping trip more efficient by organizing your list by aisle or section: produce, meat and seafood, freezer, dairy, and specialty.

- **Get inspired.** If you come across a new or unusual food (for example, maitake mushrooms or celeriac) that draws your attention, give yourself permission to add it to your basket. Make a point of learning about it, and create a dish to highlight its delicious qualities.

- **Swap as needed.** This is a pro move: Swap an ingredient for another like it that looks fresher at the market. Your recipe will turn out all the more flavorful for it.

- **Avoid overly processed foods.** As much as possible, choose whole foods that are products of nature, not food products that have been processed in a number of ways, often loaded with preservatives, artificial colors and flavors, and added sugar. Read product labels carefully and investigate unfamiliar ingredients.

- **Choose fresher, better ingredients.** Whenever possible, choose organic, fresh ingredients. Organic foods have no harmful chemicals applied to them while they grow, making them a healthier option.

- **Know your meat and fish.** Get familiar with pasture-raised meats (which means the animals lived in their natural environment and ate their natural diet, instead of being confined to a cage and fed industrialized feed). These animals have been treated more humanely than their counterparts and will be healthier. For fish, opt for wild instead of "farm-raised."

- **Find a farmers' market.** Farmers' market foods are local and fresher by nature, and shopping there supports your local community. Farmers' markets can also be a lot of fun! Farmers display their stands in unique ways, showing off the literal fruits of their labor. Feel free to ask questions, especially if they aren't busy.

- **Minimize spoilage.** Make the most of the food you bring home by using it in the order it was purchased. This is known as "first in, first out." Check expiration dates on packages, and use foods expiring soonest.

MEASURING SKILLS

While liquid and dry measuring cups hold the same volume, dry measuring cups are meant to be filled to the brim and then the excess leveled off for precision (often with the edge of a knife). Liquid measurements end below the lip of the cup or are ideally measured using a transparent glass or plastic spouted cup.

Dry Measuring

Flour should be kept in a wide-mouth jar or bag for ease. Choose a measuring cup that fits the amount you need. With a scoop or spoon, fill the cup until it overflows. Do not pack the flour down or use the measuring cup to scoop the flour, as it will cause compression. Using the straight edge of a butter knife, level the flour even with the rim of the measuring cup.

Sugar is more dense. To measure it, scoop directly using the measuring cup and shake it a couple times to settle the amount level to the cup rim. For brown sugar, scoop into the measuring cup, then pack it in with the flat of your palm until it is level with the rim. Next, tap it out into a bowl. If you packed it well, it should keep its shape.

When you fill and then level the ingredients flush with the rim, you know your measurement is correct. The same goes for measuring spoons: Scoop and sweep the excess away with a straight edge, measuring to the rim of the spoon.

Liquid Measuring

Measure liquids in a spouted, transparent measuring cup set on an even surface. Pour liquid so that it reaches the measurement line. Be sure your eyes are even with the level of the measurement. If need be, bend down to read the measurement at eye level.

homemade granola

PREP TIME
10 minutes

COOK TIME
50 minutes

MAKES

5–6
CUPS

**TOOLS /
EQUIPMENT**

Whisk

Large bowl

Small bowl

Rubber spatula

Rimmed
baking sheet

Parchment paper

Wire cooling rack

3 cups rolled oats

¾ cup raw almonds, coarsely chopped

½ cup raw hulled pumpkin, sesame,
or sunflower seeds, or a mix

¼ cup flaxseed

¼ cup quinoa or millet

¼ cup wheat bran

⅓ cup olive oil

½ cup pure maple syrup or honey

¼ cup packed light brown sugar

1 teaspoon ground cinnamon

¾ teaspoon freshly grated nutmeg

1 teaspoon flake salt, such as Maldon

1 egg white, beaten until foamy

½ cup dried cranberries, blueberries,
figs, cherries, or other dried fruit

¼ cup unsweetened coconut flakes

Preheat the oven to 300°F.

Mix the dry ingredients.
In a large bowl, mix the oats, almonds, pumpkin
seeds, flaxseed, quinoa, and bran. Set aside.

Combine with the spices and wet ingredients.
In a small bowl, use a rubber spatula to stir together
the oil, maple syrup, brown sugar, cinnamon, nutmeg,
salt, and egg white. Pour the liquid over the oat
mixture, and fold until well combined.

Bake the granola.
On a rimmed baking sheet lined with parchment
paper, spread the granola evenly. Bake for 30 to
40 minutes, stirring every 10 minutes for even
browning.

Add the fruit.
Add the dried fruit and the coconut flakes, stir to
combine, and bake until the granola is fragrant and
a beautiful, toasty brown, about 10 minutes more.

Store and serve.
Set the sheet on a cooling rack to cool completely.
Transfer the granola to jars or airtight containers,
and store at room temperature. Enjoy as a snack,
as a topping for yogurt or ice cream, or as cereal
with milk.

DID YOU KNOW? You can also make a
savory granola. Instead of maple syrup,
swap in a little cayenne or soy sauce, and
add chopped rosemary and more nuts, like
cashews, pecans, and walnuts.

USING THE STOVE

When using the stove it's important to practice safe cooking habits. Even when being careful, a kitchen fire is a real possibility. For the most part, fires are avoidable if you follow these important safety tips:

- Never leave cooking food unattended.
- Keep the stove top clean of any food, oil, or grease, which can ignite while cooking.
- Always tie back long hair (standard restaurant procedure)
- Roll up long sleeves, and remove any hanging jewelry that can get caught on burners or pan handles.

Turning on the Stove

Gas stoves have a continuously burning tiny flame called a pilot light under the cooktop. This flame lights the burners when you turn them on. To ignite the burner, turn the knob all the way, often to a spot marked "Lite," until you hear a clicking sound. Once the burner has ignited, adjust the flame to the temperature called for in the recipe.

Burners on electric stoves consist of coiled heating elements that normally range in temperature from Low (1) to High (10). The temperature is controlled by the knob. Flat, glass-ceramic cooktops are also electric, but they conduct heat in a different manner. This type of cooktop heats more quickly and also cools more quickly. Only the burner area heats up, while the adjacent cooktop remains cool. Depending on the stove, you may control the heat via a knob, or you may control the temperature digitally through a panel on the stove.

Making Sure the Pan Is Hot

The first step in stove-top cooking is heating your pan. Heat it while dry, over medium-high heat. To test the pan for readiness, sprinkle a drop of water: If the drop sizzles and jumps around, it's ready.

Adjust the flame to the specific recipe's requirements, and add your cooking oil or butter. You need only a little, as the heat will disperse it across the pan's surface area as it melts down. This will make your food less likely to stick. Heat the butter and allow it to foam—then add your food. If you are using oil, heat it until it pulls to the edge of pan, also known as when oil "smiles," and then add the food. Do not heat oil so much that it smokes; that means it has burned.

Resisting the Temptation to Fuss

Resist the urge to fuss with the food as it cooks; instead, be patient. You must give the pan—and the food—enough time to work its magic. Use the timing in the recipe as a guide for how frequently to stir or for when to turn food to the other side.

As you wait for the next step in a recipe, pay attention to how your food looks, smells, and sounds: These are cues that will make you an expert cook. Sliced onions sautéing in the pan turn from opaque to transparent. Nuts are aromatic just when they become ready during toasting. A sauce will bubble quietly once it has come to a simmer. Each detail is important, and when observed, it will give you the information you need to become a confident chef.

BURNER DOS AND DON'TS

DON'T leave a burner on that does not have a filled pot or pan on it.

DON'T leave an empty pan on a hot burner.

DON'T put a glass or ceramic pan or lid on a hot burner.

DO use appropriately sized burners for the size pot or pan you are using.

DO turn any pot or pan handle away from the edge of the stove, as it could get knocked over if turned out.

DO keep oven mitts as well as other cloth and paper goods away from stove burners.

DO assume pots and pans are hot, and handle them with dry pot holders.

DON'T hover over the pan while cooking, since food often splatters.

DO turn food away from you rather than toward you when turning food over, so any hot liquid or grease is directed away from your skin.

Stove-Top Techniques

Here are the main stove-top cooking techniques you'll use over and over again:

Simmer Liquids over high heat boil rapidly, while liquids over a lower heat simmer. Simmering is a way of gently cooking ingredients until they are tender.

After bringing your ingredients to a boil over high heat, turn the heat to low or medium-low for gentle bubbling in the pot: You should see the liquid shimmer and a bubble or two form every few seconds.

Boil Boiling means high heat and continuous bubbles popping out of vigorously moving liquid in the pot. Boiling helps keep food in motion, prevents sticking, and cooks food quickly. This process is most often used for cooking pasta and some grains, boiling eggs, and blanching vegetables.

Fry Frying is cooking food in oil over moderate to high heat. There are two basic types of frying: shallow frying and deep-frying. Shallow frying is cooking food in oil that comes up to partially cover the food. Deep-frying is cooking food by submerging it in hot oil.

Some oils are meant for cooking, others for flavor. Cooking oils have a mild flavor and scent and a high "smoke point"—the temperature at which oil starts to smoke and burn—making them ideal for frying. If the frying oil isn't hot enough, food will become soggy. If it's too hot, food will burn before fully cooking.

Butter has a low smoking point, making it a poor choice for frying. Good frying oils include canola, grapeseed, peanut, safflower, and sunflower oils.

Grill Grilling is great for many reasons: It is a fast way of cooking; few seasonings aside from olive oil, salt, and pepper are needed; and the textures of charred, juicy foods are delicious. For the purposes of this book, you'll focus on stove-top grilling using your grill pan.

HOW TO HANDLE A FIRE

In the unlikely event of a fire, turn off the burners or the oven. If the fire is small and contained in the pan, smother it with baking soda or cover it with a metal lid to extinguish it. Study the instructions on how to use an ABC or UL-rated dry chemical fire extinguisher, and keep it, baking soda, and metal lids nearby to put out fires quickly. Never use flour or fan the flames, and never use water to put out a grease fire.

Place a fire extinguisher close to an exit so you can back out of the kitchen or leave your home if the fire becomes uncontrollable. Keep a stocked first aid kit near the fire extinguisher. If you have been burned, apply ice and then aloe vera to the affected area.

If the fire cannot be extinguished, exit your home and call 911 for emergency help.

Melt Melting is the process of turning a solid into a liquid using low heat. You can melt butter or cheese in a sauce pan, but for chocolate or custards, the best method is to use a double boiler on your stove top. You can buy a double boiler, but it's easy to fashion your own. Use a tempered glass or metal mixing bowl, or small saucepan, and a larger saucepan. The bowl or small saucepan should fit into the large saucepan for best heat distribution, with only a small gap between them. To use the double boiler, add 1 to 2 inches of water to the larger pan, and place the bowl or small saucepan into it, filled with whatever you intend to melt, and bring the water to a simmer.

Sauté In sautéing, you'll move the pan or stir occasionally to keep food from sticking and to cook each piece at the same rate. Use a large, wide pan to sauté so that you don't crowd the food. This helps air circulate around each piece, allowing the heat of the pan to cook some of the natural moisture out of the food, intensifying flavors.

When you add food to the hot pan to sauté, you should hear a sizzle immediately upon contact. Oil, butter, and grease can splatter while cooking, so take extra care and lay food down gently into the pan. Cook over medium-high heat according to the recipe (until softened; until browned), and stir the food occasionally, every 30 seconds or so.

classic fried egg

PREP TIME
1 minute

COOK TIME
2–4 minutes

SERVES
1

**TOOLS /
EQUIPMENT**

Small bowl

Small cast-iron or
enameled skillet

Spatula

1 large egg

1 teaspoon olive oil or butter

Pinch sea salt (optional)

Freshly ground black pepper (optional)

HELPFUL HINT

How long you cook the egg is a
matter of personal preference.
Sunny-side up (runny yolk): no
more than 3 minutes. Over easy
(semi-solid yolk): no more than
4 minutes. Over hard (solid yolk):
5 minutes or so. To gauge "doneness," gently shake the pan to see
if the yolk jiggles.

Crack the egg.
Tap the egg firmly on the rim of a bowl to crack
it, then empty it into a small bowl. This low-stress
method helps prevent broken yolks.

Heat the skillet.
Heat a small skillet to medium temperature.

Coat the skillet.
Drizzle the olive oil (or place the butter) into the
skillet. When the oil becomes shimmery and pulls
to the edges of the skillet (or the butter sizzles),
it is ready.

Cook the egg.
Pour the egg gently into the skillet, holding the bowl
just above it for an easy transfer. You should see
the egg bubble and sizzle. If it doesn't, your pan
was not hot enough. Gently tilt the skillet to one
side and then the other, spreading the white in an
even layer to help it cook fully. Cook to your ideal
"doneness" (see Helpful Hint).

Serve.
When your fried egg is ready, turn off the burner, hold
the skillet handle with a pot holder, and with your
other hand, slide a spatula under the egg to transfer it
to a plate. Season with salt and pepper (if using), and
eat immediately. This easy, delicious, nourishing dish
works for breakfast or dinner and pairs nicely with
toast, a salad, or even pasta and veggies.

KNIFE SKILLS

The knife is probably the most commonly used tool in the kitchen and also the most important to learn how to use properly so that you avoid hurting yourself. You will develop these skills over time, but technique and the right knife for the job are key. As you practice these skills and become familiar with knives, using this essential kitchen tool will begin to feel like second nature. Cutting food doesn't just make it easier to eat, it also allows foods of different sizes to cook at the same rate and helps you create more delicious-looking dishes!

What Knife Is Best?

A knife may feel large or awkward at first—so you can ask for the help of an adult or use a mini chopper until you gain more practice. While some knives are better for certain cutting tasks than others, at this stage, I recommend choosing a knife that feels comfortable and natural in your hands.

KNIFE SAFETY RULES

1. Above all else: Always pay attention to what you are doing!

2. Always cut on a cutting board made of a material other than glass, marble, or metal to avoid slipping. Wood and plastic are good choices. Place a dampened tea towel under the cutting board to keep it in place as you cut.

3. Keep your knives sharp. If you use dull knives, you'll end up pushing harder, which may lead to an accident.

4. If you have to carry a knife from one area of the kitchen to another, always carry it point down, parallel to your side, as you walk.

5. This is not the circus. Never attempt to catch a falling knife—step back and allow it to fall. You should also wear closed-toe shoes as a precaution.

6. Never leave a knife in the sink. Anyone who reaches into the sink may not know it is there and could be injured.

Bread knife This serrated-blade knife is great for sawing through the crusty exterior of bread but is also useful for cutting tomatoes or pineapple, shaving chocolate, and more.

Chef's knife This is one of the larger of the knives you'll use in the kitchen. It works in a rocking motion and should feel comfortable in your hand. Go to a store with a wide selection, and try out different brands. Find one that feels neither too heavy nor too light and that is not too long or too short. It will become your trusted friend.

Paring knife A small paring knife is a good beginner knife, especially if you don't feel adept at holding a larger knife like a chef's knife yet. It's also great for younger kids with smaller hands. This knife is good for small chopping tasks, like trimming ends off of green beans, shaving the pith from lemon peel, skinning a tomato, or hulling strawberries.

Sharpening Knives

There is no substitute for using sharpening stones for your knives, but it's a skill that needs to be developed, even for adults. You may consider using knife-sharpening kits while you get your cutting and cooking skills up and running.

Learning to Cut

Learning to safely and efficiently make even cuts is essential to becoming a good cook. The proper way to hold a larger knife, like a chef's knife, is to grab it as if you were shaking hands: wrap your middle finger, ring finger, and pinkie finger around the handle to hold it, but then rest your index finger on one side of the blade, curling it up a little so you do not cut yourself. Rest your thumb on the opposite side, and pinch the blade between your thumb and index finger to guide it, with the other fingers holding the handle firmly. This will give you leverage and control over the knife and keep you from cutting yourself. Practice this grip to strike the right balance without holding the knife too tightly so you don't tire out your hand.

For smaller knives, like a paring knife, you use the same gripping technique. You may extend your index finger along the top of the knife for greater control.

Always use two hands when cutting. Your less dominant hand will hold the food. Make a claw shape with your fingers, curling the fingertips back (including your thumb) and sticking the knuckles out, then rest your fingertips on the food you plan to cut. As you slice, rest your knuckles against the side of the knife to steer it, make slices of equal size, and keep your fingers stable as you move up the food, keeping them out of the way of the sharp blade. Move in smooth, even strokes, using the blade's sharp edge to do the cutting rather than forcing the blade through the food.

PRACTICE ROUND: CUTTING CELERY

1. Place the curved side of a celery stalk up and the flat edges down to stabilize the food on the cutting board.

2. Get your holding hand "claw" in place, and with the chef's knife in your other hand, place the tip of your knife on the cutting board.

3. As you cut, the tip of your knife should not leave the cutting board but should stay anchored there, pivoting as you smoothly work with the knife.

4. Move ¼ inch onto the celery, and with a sliding motion, make a cut.

5. You did it!

Use the same practice to continue cutting the whole stalk. As you cut, the chopped pieces may cling to the knife. It is helpful to pause after a few slices to brush them off and reposition your holding hand, moving farther up the food as you continue to make slices.

Cutting Styles

With any of these methods, first trim veggies and fruit of any unwanted things like stems, cores, and roots. You may also need to cut a sliver off any round or wobbly vegetable or halve it to stabilize it on the cutting board as you slice or chop.

A **Chop** To cut items into small pieces uniformly. It doesn't mean to hack the food up but to create an emphasis on same-size pieces.

B **Dice** To cut items into small cubes. You first cut the food into long, equal-size, matchstick-shaped pieces (see Julienne), then chop those into whatever size dice is called for in the recipe.

C **Julienne** To cut foods into long, thin strips, like matchsticks.

D **Mince** To cut into very small pieces. Mincing requires the use of your holding hand to keep the tip of the knife in place as you rock the blade back and forth across the food.

E **Slice** To cut broad, thin pieces and can be the finished cut or the first step in creating other cuts.

PREP TIME
15 minutes

COOK TIME
none

SERVES
4

TOOLS / EQUIPMENT

Large bowl

Rubber gloves or plastic bag

Citrus reamer

2 large tomatoes

1 small white or red onion

1 jalapeño pepper

½ cup fresh cilantro

1 lime

¼ teaspoon cumin

Flake salt, such as Maldon

Freshly ground black pepper

delicious additions

Diced fresh mango, pineapple, or jicama

Chopped tomatillos or cucumbers

Minced chipotle or poblano pepper

Prepare the tomatoes.
Dice the tomatoes and transfer them, along with any juices, from the cutting board into a large bowl.

Prepare the onion.
Peel and trim the onion and mince it, rocking the knife back and forth, until it is almost the size of confetti. Use the side of the knife to scrape the onion into the bowl with the tomatoes.

Clean your tools.
Rinse the knife and board under cold water, and wipe dry if the sharp onion juices have made you tear up.

Prepare the pepper.
Wearing a rubber glove or a plastic bag secured with a rubber band around your wrist, slice the jalapeño in half lengthwise. Remove the core and seeds, and discard. Mince the jalapeño, and add it to the bowl. Remove the glove or plastic bag and discard.

Prepare the cilantro.
Chop the cilantro, and add it to the mixture.

Prepare the lime.
Slice a lime in half widthwise, and squeeze its juice over the mixture in the bowl.

Combine the ingredients.
Stir, adding cumin, and salt and pepper to taste. Taste and add more salt or lime juice if needed. Refrigerate for 15 minutes, up to 1 hour, to let the flavors meld.

PREP WORK

As the headline implies, you must do work in preparation to cook a recipe so that you'll be ready to execute each step as needed. The difference between harmony and a disaster often lies in how well you have prepared. If you measure, slice and dice, and get all the ingredients ready in advance, then lay them out in order of use *before* getting into the cooking, you will guarantee a less stressful experience.

Beating

To beat an egg, crack it into a bowl. Use a whisk to stir vigorously in a circular motion to break the yolk and combine it with the whites. Beating also brings air into a mixture, creating volume. Beat lightly or well to incorporate the mixture, depending on what the specific recipe calls for. This common technique is used when making scrambled eggs, omelets, cakes, mayonnaise, and meringue.

Mixing

To mix, use a rubber spatula or wooden spoon to stir ingredients together. It may be dry or wet ingredients you are asked to mix, and depending on their respective thicknesses, mixing may either take a moment or require a few minutes to incorporate.

Separating Eggs

Cold eggs are easier to separate. Crack an egg on the lip of a bowl or on a flat surface. Open the egg over the bowl, and allow the yolk to settle in its shell. Carefully transfer the yolk back and forth from one shell half to the other. The slippery white will drip into the bowl. Transfer the yolk into another bowl. If separating more than one egg, use a third bowl to pour successfully separated whites into so that if any yolk drips into your egg-separating bowl as you go, you can discard without contaminating all the egg whites.

After cracking an egg, you can also cup your hand over a small bowl and pour the yolk into it. Allow the thick white to seep between your fingers and drop into the bowl as you separate them slightly, leaving the yolk in your palm. Slip the egg yolk into a bowl designated for yolks, transfer the white into a larger bowl reserved for whites, and repeat until you have enough for the recipe. This method lets you really "get into" your food! If you choose this version, wash your hands thoroughly before and after handling the eggs.

Separated eggs are incorporated into recipes from meringues (whites) to aioli (yolks).

Peeling

Allow the small end of the vegetable to rest on the cutting board, holding it at a slight angle at the other end or from underneath. With the other hand, use fluid movements to glide the peeler along the vegetable away from you, in a top-down motion, rotating the vegetable as you go, until you return to where you started. Flip the vegetable so that the bottom is now the top, and repeat on any missed areas until the vegetable is fully peeled.

If no harmful chemicals were used to grow your vegetables and the skins aren't very tough, you don't have to peel them. Plus, that is where much of the nutrition lives. Pesticide-free veggies just need to be scrubbed free of dirt under cold running water.

Juicing

Use a citrus reamer to juice whole lemons, limes, oranges, and other citrus fruits. First, roll the fruit back and forth along the surface of the counter with your palm while gently pressing down. This breaks down some of the fibers, making the juice easier to extract.

Lay the fruit on its side, tip-end and stem-end parallel to each other. Hold one end, and slice it in half down the middle. Position the cut side over a bowl to catch the juice. Hold the fruit cupped in one hand, and press the pointed mound of the reamer into the fruit with the other, twisting the reamer back and forth to get all the juice out.

Another way to juice is by using a citrus reamer mounted in a bowl. Here, the reamer remains stationary. Twist the fruit back and forth on its ridges, pressing gently down as you do so to extract the juice. Some versions of this type of reamer include a sieve-catch in the bowl with an additional compartment beneath it to easily separate the seeds and pulp from the juice.

If you don't have a citrus reamer, you can use a fork and achieve the same results. Use the tines of a fork as you would a handheld reamer, but alternate twisting the fork, then the fruit, to extract the most juice.

If you only need a small amount of citrus juice, cut a wedge from the fruit, saving the rest (up to three days) in a sealed container in the refrigerator. To squeeze a little lemon juice to season a dish, cut a wedge from the lemon, then, holding one hand underneath it to catch any seeds, squeeze the wedge over your food.

Citrus juice is a universally used flavor; use it for salads and soups, in drinks, on cooked meat, fish, and grains—anytime you want a little extra zing.

Mincing or Pressing Garlic

You can choose to mince garlic with a knife or use a garlic press if you have one on hand. For speedy results, grate garlic on a zester to get a fine texture that will cook evenly.

Grating and Zesting

Box graters have four sides, each with different-size blades: zesting (the finest), shredding, grating, and slicing. To grate cheese or vegetables on a box grater, position the grater over a dish or bowl to collect the shredded results. Hold the grater handle, and press down to stabilize it. Hold the vegetable at one end and run it top-down along the grater, so that the blades catch the edge of the veggie to grate it.

The blades of box graters are very sharp and can cut you; as you grate food, be careful to reposition your hand further up the food, keeping a safe distance between your knuckles and the sharp edges. It is nearly impossible to grate the last end of the food without cutting yourself, so save the last bit to use for stock or discard it.

Many recipes often call for citrus zest, or the skin of a citrus fruit minced finely. If possible, find unwaxed, organic citrus, and wash and pat them dry beforehand. Use a zester, like a Microplane. Hold the handle, and position its end down against the cutting board surface to stabilize it. You can also rest the zester teeth-up over a bowl and press the top and handle ends onto the opposite sides of the bowl, zesting directly into your recipe rather than transferring the zest from the cutting board.

Hold the citrus fruit with your other hand and, pressing moderately, move in short strokes in the opposite direction of the teeth, grating the topmost colored skin only. The white part underneath the skin, called the "pith," is bitter and unpleasant. Check after a few strokes to see if you have exposed the pith, then rotate the fruit, moving it to zest the skin in a new spot. Repeat until you have fully zested the fruit, or until you have enough for the specific recipe.

CLEANLINESS AND SAFETY

Be serious about cleanliness. Wash your hands thoroughly when handling food. Never prepare food directly on the countertop. Use cutting boards or plastic cutting mats, incorporating different ones for preparing different types of foods—one for raw fruits and veggies and a different one for raw meats. Wash cutting boards in hot, soapy water and then pat or air dry, and wipe down counters with hot water.

Keep hot foods hot and cold foods cold. Check the temperature of your refrigerator. It should be set to 40°F (5°C). Your freezer should be set to 0°F (−18°C) or lower. These chilly temperatures will keep your food from spoiling.

Refrigerate leftover cooked food as soon as possible to prevent the spread of bacteria. Eat leftovers within 3 to 4 days. Food left at temperatures between 40 and 140ºF will spoil quickly and can carry bacteria that transmit food-borne illnesses.

bacon-herb frittata sandwich

PREP TIME
10 minutes

COOK TIME
25 minutes

SERVES
4

**TOOLS /
EQUIPMENT**

Box grater

Medium bowl

Whisk

Large skillet

Tongs

Rubber spatula

Small bowl

5 eggs

2 scallions, finely chopped

⅓ cup buttermilk

2 tablespoons crème fraîche

¼ teaspoon freshly grated nutmeg

⅛ teaspoon cayenne pepper

1 cup grated sharp Cheddar or
Swiss cheese , divided

Kosher salt

Freshly ground black pepper

3 slices bacon, cut into half-inch strips

3 whole-grain tortillas

3 tablespoons chopped fresh parsley,
to top, plus a handful of chopped salad
greens such as arugula or mesclun mix

Preheat the oven to 425°F.

Mix the eggs, spices, liquids, and cheese.
In a medium bowl, whisk together the eggs, scallions, buttermilk, crème fraîche, nutmeg, cayenne, and half the cheese. Season with salt and pepper.

Cook the bacon.
In a skillet large enough to fit the tortillas, cook the bacon until crisp over medium heat, stirring occasionally, about 6 minutes. Using tongs, transfer the bacon to the egg-scallion mixture. Pour all but a spoonful of the rendered fat into a small bowl.

Cook the tortillas.
Add 1 tortilla to the fat in the skillet and toast over medium heat, about 5 minutes. Flip halfway through to toast both sides. Transfer to a plate. Repeat with the reserved fat and remaining tortillas. Leave the last toasted tortilla in the skillet.

Cook the frittata.
Pour half of the egg mixture over the tortilla, and on medium heat, gently stir the mixture with a rubber spatula for about 30 seconds as the eggs begin to set. Add a second tortilla, followed by the rest of the egg mixture, and stir gently again for another 10 seconds or so. Top with the final tortilla and sprinkle remaining cheese on top. Transfer the skillet to the oven to bake for 8 to 10 minutes, until the frittata is puffed and golden.

Finish and serve.
Remove from the oven, top with the parsley and greens, cut into wedges, and serve warm.

BAKING SKILLS

Baked goods can be quite straightforward to make, but to bake, you must be more precise than when you cook. Baking measurements are precise for a reason: The proportions of ingredients perform a special chemistry in the finished baked goods, such as the proper rise in a crusty loaf of bread, a flaky crumb in the perfect pie, or the silky creaminess in a frosting. Pay close attention as you bake, and you will learn to make treats everyone drools over.

Oven Safety

Before preheating, check the oven for anything inside and position the racks as you need them. You should avoid storing things in the oven to reduce the risk of fire.

When opening the oven, move back from the initial blast of heat before reaching in to handle a pan so the hot air doesn't hit you in the face. Use pot holders to remove your food and close the oven door immediately afterward. Place the hot pan on a wire cooling rack, a pot holder, or a trivet.

If you discover a fire in the oven, keep the door closed and turn the oven off. Do not open the oven door until the pot or pan has completely cooled.

Creaming Butter and Sugar

Creaming butter and sugar is one of the first steps to making delicious baked goods. Use room-temperature butter (which is still solid, but if you pressed your thumb into it, it would leave a dent). Allow 30 to 60 minutes for it to soften on the countertop. With a handheld or stand mixer on low speed, beat the butter smooth for 10 to 20 seconds. Gradually pour in the sugar, and continue to beat at moderate speed, scraping the sides of the bowl periodically with a rubber spatula.

It should take 2 to 5 minutes to properly cream them together (depending on which mixer you use), resulting in a fluffy, smooth, pale yellow mixture. The mixer beats air in, and that air suspended in the mixture helps create a light texture in cakes and muffins and makes cookies light and crisp instead of hard and dense.

Cutting in Butter

"Cutting in" means incorporating butter into flour in such a way that little lumps of the butter remain whole in the mixture. When the dough is baked, these small lumps create separation in the structure of the crust, creating a flaky texture. Use unsalted butter; this will allow you to control the amount of salt in the overall recipe. When you cut butter into flour, start with the required amount cut into smaller cubes, and keep it very cold.

There are a couple of ways to incorporate butter and flour together. Before specialty tools existed, using two knives to literally cut butter into the flour was standard. You can still do it that way, though it takes patience, as the process is slow going.

A more common and faster method is to use a food processor. Pulse the processor in brief spurts to incorporate the very cold cubed butter into the measured flour. The risk in using this machine is that you could overwork the flour, stiffening the gluten in it and making it tough, not tender. There is also less control in creating those ideal pea-size bits of butter. Be conservative and pulse in fewer, short bursts. You can pulse more if needed, but you cannot go back once you have overworked it. Just like everything else with cooking and baking, if you choose this method and do it regularly, it will become more natural.

Using a Rolling Pin

Once you make pastry, do not attempt to use it immediately. The pastry is stickier and therefore harder to roll at this point. It benefits from mellowing in the refrigerator for at least 20 minutes. When the dough is ready, use a rolling pin to flatten the dough on an even surface.

Here are some tips for successfully rolling out dough:

- Sprinkle only a small amount of flour onto your work surface; too much flour will cause the dough to become dry and tough.
- Place even pressure on the rolling pin as you work; roll from the center of the pastry toward you to the edge, stopping just before rolling over the edge.

- Give a one-eighth turn to the pastry with each pass of the rolling pin so that you aren't overextending your reach.
- Roll, turn, and repeat until your dough is the required thickness.
- Patch any cracks in the dough rather than rerolling the crust; over-handling will make the dough tough.
- Work gently but quickly. If the dough becomes too warm (denting or smearing rather than spreading), refrigerate it before rolling it again. To plan for this, roll pastry out on lightly floured parchment paper, using that as your "work surface." This makes it easy to transfer pastry to chill.

Keeping Pastry Cold

Before mixing, butter needs to remain as cold as possible so that once in the hot oven, its water content can release steam, which is what creates air pockets and a flaky crust. The same is true for pastry, as it has the butter suspended throughout it. Uncooked pastry becomes flabby and stretchy when it is not cold enough, making it difficult to work with.

There's no such thing as pastry that's too cold before being baked. You can even place a fully formed, ready-to-go pie or tart into the freezer for a while to make sure it'll hold its shape once met with the blazing-hot oven. The old adage is true: "Cold with the making, hot with the baking."

Even Baking

Position cake pans or muffin tins as close to the center of the oven as possible. They should not touch each other or the oven walls. If your oven isn't wide enough to put pans side by side, place them on different racks and stagger them to allow air to circulate.

Every oven is hotter in a certain area; for example, maybe the back is hotter than the front. If you don't correct for that, you may end up with unevenly cooked pastries. To account for this, rotate your pans halfway through the process. If you are using more than one rack, also switch pan position when you rotate. However, do not open the oven constantly to check on progress. This will lower the temperature and alter the baking time.

Bake pies on the lowest oven rack, on a preheated baking sheet to prevent soggy bottom crusts. For double-crust fruit and meat pies, cut slits in the top crust or use decorative cutters to allow steam to escape. This ensures an evenly baked final creation. If crust edges brown too quickly during the long bake time, loosely fold 2-inch-wide strips of foil and press them around the edges of the crust until it's time to remove the pie from the oven.

Checking for Doneness

To test a baked good like a cake or muffin for doneness, insert a toothpick or wooden skewer into the center—it should come out clean. Cake should spring back when lightly touched and should be just pulling away from the sides of the pan.

For fruit pies to thicken properly, they need to be hot enough for the filling to boil. If your pie isn't bubbling, it isn't ready yet.

Cookies will continue to set from the heat of the pan after being removed from the oven. Remove the cookie tray, close the oven, and place the tray on your stove top. Slide the edge of a spatula under the edge of one cookie and lift gently. If the cookie stays flat across the bottom without bending or breaking in the middle, it's ready to come out.

If you prefer soft cookies, slightly underbake them or substitute brown sugar for some or all of the granulated sugar in the recipe. In many instances, this will produce softer cookies because brown sugar contains more moisture.

PREP TIME
20 minutes,
plus 40 minutes
to chill

COOK TIME
15 minutes

MAKES
2
**DOZEN
COOKIES**

**TOOLS /
EQUIPMENT**

Medium sieve
for sifting

2 large bowls

Electric mixer

Rubber spatula

Baking sheets

Wire cooling rack

Parchment paper

1 ¾ cups all-purpose flour

¼ cup flax meal

1 tablespoon finely chopped fresh
rosemary

¾ teaspoon sea salt

2 sticks unsalted butter, at room
temperature

½ cup confectioners' sugar, sifted

Mix the dry ingredients.
In a large bowl, mix the flour, flax meal, rosemary, and salt until well combined. Set aside.

Cream the butter.
In another large bowl, use an electric mixer to cream the butter, about 4 minutes. Add the sugar and blend until fluffy, scraping down the sides with a spatula.

Form the dough.
Add the flour mixture to the butter mixture, and blend on low, just until a dough forms. Test by squeezing the dough between your fingers—if it holds together, it's ready. Working quickly, roughly squeeze dough into a cylindrical shape. Wrap the parchment over it and roll dough back and forth into an even, solid roll, about 12 inches long. The ends should be the same thickness as the center.

Chill the dough.
Refrigerate the dough log for 20 minutes.

Preheat the oven to 350°F.

Cut the cookies and bake them.
Remove the dough from the refrigerator, and un-wrap the parchment paper. Use a sharp knife to cut the dough into ¼-inch-thick disks. Arrange them on baking sheets and refrigerate until firm, about 20 minutes. Bake for 15 minutes, or until the edges and bottoms are golden.

Serve.
Transfer the cookies onto a wire cooling rack to cool fully. Cookies will keep for 4 days between layers of parchment, sealed, at room temperature.

ROASTING SKILLS

Roasting is a wonderful way to prepare food and is one of the oldest cooking methods in history! Besides the convenience of putting food in the oven and walking away rather than standing at attention cooking at the stove, the flavors and texture produced by roasting transform ingredients in a most delicious way. Roasted squash makes you think it's candy; roasted potatoes become crisp *and* fluffy; roasted fish is made buttery and flaky. As long as you pay attention toward the end of the cooking cycle—neither burning nor drying out the dish—roasting foods is an easy path to yummy eating.

Opt for Pasture-Raised Meat

Pasture-raised—and some organic—meats come from animals that are treated humanely. These chickens, pigs, and cows live outside rather than in confining cages, and they eat what would be natural for them. This diet honors the animal and makes their cuts more flavorful.

When animals are fed organic feed, that also means they ate no genetically modified ingredients (GMOs) such as corn and soy, which have chemicals inserted into their seeds or genes to tolerate heavy doses of pesticides as they grow. Pasture-raised or grass-fed meats are widely available at farmers' markets, as well as at green grocers. These meats cost more, but when you buy them, you support humane animal farming.

Handling Meat

When you bring your raw meat home to cook, here's how to safely handle it:

- Never prepare raw meat, poultry, or fish where it can come into contact with cooked foods or raw vegetables—this is known as "cross-contamination prevention."
- Wash your hands if they come into contact with raw meat, poultry, or fish.
- Designate one cutting board for raw meat, poultry, and fish.
- Never put cooked food on an unwashed dish that held raw meat, poultry, or fish.

- Plan ahead: Thaw meat, poultry, and fish in the refrigerator.
- Pat dry raw meat, poultry, and fish with paper towels before cooking. Immediately dispose of the used towels.
- Cook poultry until the juices run clear.
- Use a meat thermometer to tell whether meats are cooked properly.

Food Storage

In the refrigerator, store raw meats in a pan or bag so meat juices don't drip onto other foods. Smell the meat before you begin to work with it: If it has a strong, unpleasant, or "off" odor, do not use it. Freeze or cook raw ground meat, fish, and poultry within three days. Freeze or cook steaks, roasts, and chops within five days.

USING A MEAT THERMOMETER

Insert the stem end of the meat thermometer in the thickest portion of the meat, away from any bones. Cooking times may vary from oven to oven and based on meat thickness, so use a meat thermometer to make sure food has reached a safe minimum internal temperature. Wash the stem between uses.

Always allow meat to rest before cutting into it. You will retain internal juices better by resting meat fresh out of the pan, grill, or oven for at least 10 minutes (up to 20 minutes for larger cuts) under a piece of aluminum foil bent into a tent-like shape. This keeps your meat warm while retaining that glorious crust the cooking produced. The juicy steak or roast this technique produces is a definite sign of a skilled chef!

MEAT	INTERNAL TEMPERATURE	INTERNALLY, MEAT LOOKS LIKE
Beef, whole cuts (steaks, roasts, and chops), medium rare	120°F to 130°F	Deep pink, juicy
Beef, whole cuts (steaks, roasts, and chops), medium	140°F	Pink
Ground beef, pork, and lamb	160°F	Light pink
Lamb, whole cuts (steaks, roasts, and chops), medium rare	120°F to 130°F	Deep pink, juicy
Lamb, whole cuts (steaks, roasts, and chops), medium	140°F	Pink
Pork, whole cuts (roasts and chops), medium	145°F	Light pink
Poultry, whole, pieces	165°F	White, no red meat

PREP TIME
10 minutes

COOK TIME
35 minutes

SERVES
4

TOOLS / EQUIPMENT

Large cast-iron skillet

Wooden spoon

Tongs

4 sweet Italian or bratwurst sausage links, uncooked

4 small Granny Smith or Braeburn apples, cored and cut into wedges

5 shallots, peeled and sliced into wedges

1 handful fresh sage leaves, torn

2 tablespoons olive oil

Kosher salt

Freshly ground black pepper

½ cup apple cider vinegar

Dijon or grain mustard, for serving

Salad greens (optional), for serving

Crusty bread (optional), for serving

Preheat the oven to 425°F.

Pat the sausages dry with a paper towel.

Roast the apple mixture.
In a large cast-iron skillet, toss the apples, shallots, and sage in the olive oil, and season with salt and pepper. Transfer to the oven, and roast for 15 minutes.

Add the sausage, and continue cooking.
Using pot holders, remove the skillet from the oven, and use tongs to turn the roasted apple mixture. Nestle the sausages in between. Roast until the sausage is browned and cooked through and the apple mixture is tender and caramelized, 15 to 20 minutes more.

Serve.
Add the apple cider vinegar to the pan, and use a wooden spoon to scrape up any browned bits, letting it bubble. Bring the skillet tableside, and set it on a trivet. Serve at once alongside your favorite mustard, a pile of greens, and crusty bread (if using) to mop up the juices.

YOU MADE IT!

Congratulations! You learned how to read a recipe, measure ingredients, use the stove, cut and prep ingredients, and bake and roast—and along the way, you built your confidence in the kitchen!

Maybe you had some hiccups and didn't master a lesson as well as you hoped to. Try the recipe tutorials again and study as you go. When you understand what went wrong the first time and persist—taking the time to do it right—the better your skills will be when you encounter new recipes that use the same techniques.

The following chapters are some of the most exciting: you get to pick recipes to cook! If you want to ease in, start with simpler recipes and work your way up. Here are some recipe suggestions:

IT'S A CINCH

SHOW YOUR SAVVY

FEELING BOLD

PART TWO
recipes

Dutch Baby (page 76)

3

breakfast

simple scrambled eggs

PREP TIME
5 minutes

COOK TIME
5–10 minutes

SERVES
4

**TOOLS /
EQUIPMENT**

Small bowl

Whisk

Medium sauté pan

Heat-tolerant
rubber spatula

6 to 8 eggs

Kosher salt

Freshly ground black pepper

4 tablespoons butter

Flake salt, such as Maldon, for finishing

delicious additions

Sautéed broccoli or mushrooms

*Shredded cheese, folded in or
finely shredded to top*

Minced scallions or chives

Diced tomatoes

Bacon or ham

Beat the eggs.
Crack the eggs into a small bowl, and whisk until
frothy. Season with salt and pepper.

Add the eggs to the pan.
Melt the butter in a medium sauté pan over
medium heat, and then turn the heat to low as the
butter foams. Pour the eggs in and let sit for a few
seconds.

Cook the eggs.
Use a spatula to nudge and stir the eggs, scraping
the bottom continuously as you move them around
the pan to help prevent sticking. Use the spatula to
push the eggs from center-out, and then scrape the
pan edge, swirling the outermost eggs into the center. Keep doing this until the eggs begin to look like
pudding and then form into dense, rich egg curds,
about 4 minutes.

Serve.
Remove the pan from the heat while the eggs are
still a little loose; they will continue to cook on the
way from the pan to your plate. Sprinkle with a little
flake salt and pepper, and eat at once.

> HELPFUL HINT You want the eggs to cook
> slowly, so if they start sticking, turn your
> heat even lower and keep stirring; not fast, but
> continuously.

cheesy egg sandwich

PREP TIME
5 minutes

COOK TIME
10 minutes

SERVES
4

TOOLS / EQUIPMENT

Bread knife

Box grater

Toaster oven

Small cast-iron skillet

Metal spatula

Olive oil, for drizzling and frying

1 baguette or other crusty bread, sliced into 5-inch sections and halved horizontally

⅔ cup grated sharp Cheddar cheese, divided

4 eggs

1 handful greens (arugula or spinach) per person, rinsed and patted dry

Sea salt

Freshly ground black pepper

Toast the bread.
Drizzle a little olive oil onto the cut sides of the bread, and lay the slices on a toaster tray. Toast until golden and crispy, about 3 minutes. Turn the slices cut-side up, transfer to plates, and sprinkle the cheese evenly on the toast.

Melt the cheese.
Return the bread to the toaster oven and broil until the cheese bubbles, about 5 minutes. Carefully transfer the toast to the plates.

Fry the eggs.
In a small cast-iron skillet over medium-high heat, fry the eggs in enough olive oil to coat the pan once it is hot. Turn the heat to medium after 1 minute, allowing the whites to cook fully while keeping the yolks soft. Season with salt and pepper.

Serve.
Pile the greens onto the toast sandwich bottoms, followed by the fried egg; then top with broiled cheesy toast. Eat at once, with a plate underneath to catch any drips of liquidy golden yolk.

> **TRY INSTEAD** This recipe has many options! Swap sautéed spinach for the fresh greens, or pepper Jack cheese for the Cheddar. Add mustard, mayonnaise or avocado. Add a sausage patty or ham.

breakfast burrito bar

PREP TIME
10 minutes

COOK TIME
12 minutes

SERVES
4

TOOLS / EQUIPMENT

Different-size festive bowls

Dish towel

Box grater

Colander

Sauté pan

Aluminum foil

4 to 8 whole-grain (8- or 10-inch) tortillas

6 to 8 eggs, scrambled

2 cups canned black beans, drained and rinsed

3 strips cooked bacon, crumbled

1 cup Greek yogurt or sour cream

1 cup bite-size cilantro sprigs

1½ cups Salsa Fresca (page 46)

½ cup orange, red, or green bell peppers, diced

1½ cups shredded sharp Cheddar or Monterey Jack cheese

1½ cups diced avocado or No-Nonsense Guacamole (page 101)

Sriracha or Cholula hot sauce, for garnish

Preheat the oven to 375°F.

Warm the tortillas.

Wrap a stack of 4 tortillas in aluminum foil and warm for 5 to 10 minutes. If you are preparing 8 tortillas, make 2 wrapped bundles. Wrap the warmed foil bundles in a dish towel to keep them toasty.

Serve.

Serve the fillings and toppings in festive, colorful bowls. Arrange them together on the table or counter, along with the towel-wrapped tortillas, and allow your guests to assemble their own burrito creations.

DID YOU KNOW? Many burrito bar items can be made ahead and refrigerated, such as the salsa, No-Nonsense Guacamole, and diced pepper mix.

shakshuka (tomato-egg bake)

PREP TIME
10 minutes

COOK TIME
20 minutes

SERVES

4

TOOLS / EQUIPMENT

Toaster oven

Mortar and pestle

Large enameled skillet

Wooden spoon

1 onion, chopped

2 tablespoons olive oil

2 garlic cloves, chopped

1 (28-ounce) can tomatoes, or Homemade Tomato Sauce (page 134)

1 tablespoon za'atar

2 teaspoons cumin seeds, toasted and ground in a mortar and pestle (see No-Nonsense Guacamole recipe, page 101)

Kosher salt

Freshly ground black pepper

4 eggs

¼ cup fresh cilantro leaves, for garnish

⅔ cup Greek yogurt or sour cream

Crusty bread, torn, for serving

delicious additions

Chickpeas
Artichoke hearts
Feta

Preheat the oven to 375°F.

Cook the onion and garlic.
In a large enameled skillet over medium heat, sauté the onion in olive oil for 3 to 5 minutes. Add the chopped garlic, and cook for another minute.

Add the tomatoes and aromatics.
Add the tomatoes, and bring to a simmer. Add the za'atar and cumin, season with salt and pepper, and simmer uncovered for a few minutes, until the sauce thickens. Break the tomatoes into chunks using the edge of a wooden spoon. Taste and adjust seasoning as needed.

Add the eggs.
Use the wooden spoon to make four nests in the sauce and crack an egg into each. Season the eggs with salt and pepper, and transfer the skillet to the oven, cooking for 7 to 10 minutes, or until the eggs are just set.

Serve.
Serve from the skillet on a trivet at the table. Season with salt and pepper to taste, and garnish with fresh cilantro and a few dollops of yogurt. Serve with the bread to mop up the sauce and yolks.

DID YOU KNOW? This one-skillet dish originated in North Africa; *shakshuka* means "a mixture."

savory sausage hash

PREP TIME
15 minutes

COOK TIME
15 minutes

SERVES
4

**TOOLS /
EQUIPMENT**

Large enameled or
cast-iron skillet

Fine grater

Wooden spoon

2 tablespoons olive oil, divided

1 onion, finely chopped

3 Yukon gold potatoes, scrubbed and
diced into ½-inch cubes

1 pound hot or Italian pork sausage,
casings removed

2 garlic cloves, finely grated

1 small jalapeño, cored and seeded,
finely chopped

2 tablespoons minced fresh rosemary

1 teaspoon dried smoked paprika

Sea salt

Freshly ground black pepper

Cook the onion and potatoes.

Place a large skillet over medium heat, and add
1 tablespoon of olive oil when the pan is hot. Add
the onion and sauté for 5 minutes, or until they
become translucent, stirring occasionally. Add the
potatoes and the remaining 1 tablespoon of olive
oil, and stir to incorporate. Sauté the mixture for
another 5 minutes, stirring only a few times during
this step so the potatoes can form a nice crust.

Cook the sausage.

Add the sausage, garlic, and jalapeño, and brown
the meat, crumbling it into smaller pieces with the
edge of a wooden spoon. Add the rosemary and
paprika, and season with salt and pepper. Stirring
occasionally, lower the heat if needed as you cook
the mixture, until the potatoes become crispy and
fork tender and the meat is browned all over.

Serve.

Serve from the skillet on a trivet at the table.

spiced-orange french toast

PREP TIME
10 minutes

COOK TIME
20 minutes

SERVES
4

**TOOLS /
EQUIPMENT**

Citrus reamer

Zester

Shallow
baking dish

Large cast-
iron skillet

Metal spatula

5 eggs

1⅓ cup whole milk

2 tablespoons fresh-squeezed
orange juice

Zest of 1 orange

1 teaspoon ground cinnamon

Sea salt

1 tablespoon butter, plus more as
needed for the pan and for serving

1 tablespoon grapeseed oil, plus
more as needed

8 (½-inch-thick) slices brioche
or challah bread

Maple syrup, for serving

Whisk the ingredients.

In a shallow baking dish, use a fork to beat together
the eggs, milk, juice, zest, cinnamon, and a large
pinch of salt.

Prepare to cook the French toast.

In a large cast-iron skillet over medium heat, heat
the butter and grapeseed oil. Dip the brioche one
slice at a time into the egg mixture to coat, punc-
turing it a couple of times with a fork. Don't let
the bread sit in the custard for very long, as it will
become soggy.

Pan fry in batches.

When the butter foams, carefully place the bread
into the skillet, two slices at a time. Pan fry the bread
in batches until golden brown on both sides, flipping
when one side is done, about 5 minutes per batch.
Repeat with the remaining slices, adding more butter
and oil to the pan as needed.

Serve.

Serve the French toast warm with butter and
maple syrup.

HELPFUL HINT Always zest citrus before
you juice it. It's much easier to hold onto
the fruit before its juice has been squeezed.

PRO TIP Keep cooked French toast
warm on a baking sheet in a 300°F
oven as you cook the rest.

dutch baby

PREP TIME
5 minutes

COOK TIME
15 minutes

SERVES

4

**TOOLS /
EQUIPMENT**

Small, shallow
ramekins

Baking sheet

Blender

¾ cup all-purpose flour

¾ cup whole milk

4 eggs, lightly beaten

2 tablespoons cane sugar

Pinch freshly grated nutmeg

¼ teaspoon sea salt

4 tablespoons butter, divided
into 4 pats

Confectioners' sugar, for dusting

Lemon wedges, for serving

delicious additions

Jam

Cinnamon sugar

Fresh berries

Stewed apples

Whipped cream or crème fraîche

Preheat the oven to 425°F.

Prep the ramekins.
Arrange the ramekins on a rimmed baking sheet,
and place in the oven to heat.

Blend the ingredients.
In a blender, mix the flour, milk, eggs, sugar, nutmeg,
and salt until frothy.

Butter the ramekins.
When the ramekins are hot, add a pat of butter to
each and, using pot holders for protection, swirl
to coat. Butter should foam. Replace in oven until
fully melted.

Bake the Dutch Babies.
Remove baking sheet from the oven. Divide the batter
evenly among the ramekins, and bake until the Dutch
Babies are puffed and golden brown, 10 to 15 minutes.

Serve.
Working quickly while the pancakes are still puffy,
transfer the ramekins to larger plates. At the table,
sprinkle a little confectioners' sugar on top, followed
by a squeeze of lemon. Eat immediately.

DID YOU KNOW? This custardy pancake
puffs up in a delightful way as it cooks. It
also deflates quickly once out of the oven,
perfect for absorbing a final pat of butter and
some freshly squeezed citrus. For the tastiest
results, eat it right away!

banana-maple breakfast quinoa

PREP TIME
10 minutes

COOK TIME
5 minutes

SERVES
4

TOOLS / EQUIPMENT

Medium glass bowl with lid

Fine grater

Medium saucepan

Heat-tolerant rubber spatula

1 cup red or golden quinoa

2 cups almond or cashew milk, plus more for drizzling

½ teaspoon ground cinnamon

¼ teaspoon freshly grated nutmeg

¾ cup fresh or frozen blueberries

Pinch kosher salt

2 bananas

Maple syrup, for serving

Soak the quinoa overnight.

Transfer the quinoa to a glass bowl or container with a lid. Add the nut milk, cinnamon, and nutmeg. Soak on the counter overnight, lid slightly askew.

The next morning, heat the quinoa.

In a medium saucepan over medium-low heat, add the frozen berries and a pinch of salt to the quinoa mixture and warm, about 5 minutes. Have a few tablespoons of water or more nut milk nearby to drizzle in case the quinoa sticks as you stir. If using fresh berries, add them when the porridge is almost warm enough to eat.

Serve.

Spoon the quinoa into bowls, and slice bananas on top. If you like, add more freshly grated nutmeg and a dash of cinnamon. At the table, drizzle maple syrup over the top and eat at once.

> **TRY INSTEAD** Fresh-grated ginger added to the overnight soak makes this dish peppery and bright. You can also try other fruit. Swap diced apples or pears or a handful of grapes cut in half in for the berries.

open sesame nut bars

PREP TIME
10 minutes

COOK TIME
25 minutes

TOTAL TIME
1 hour 5 minutes

MAKES
16
BARS

TOOLS / EQUIPMENT

8-inch-square glass baking dish

Parchment paper

Large bowl

Small bowl

Rubber spatula

Wire cooling rack

Butter, for greasing

1¼ cups white and/or black sesame seeds

¾ cup unsweetened shredded coconut

½ cup dried apricots, chopped

¼ teaspoon sea salt

¼ cup honey

⅓ cup crunchy peanut butter

¼ teaspoon pure vanilla extract

DID YOU KNOW? These tasty, energy-boosting bars can be made three days ahead.

Preheat the oven to 350°F.

Prep the baking dish.
Butter an 8-inch-square glass baking dish, and line it with parchment paper long enough so that it extends beyond the dish by at least 2 inches on all sides. Cut slits at the corners so the parchment lays flat.

Mix the ingredients.
In a large bowl, mix together the sesame seeds, coconut, apricots, and salt. In a small bowl, stir the honey, peanut butter, and vanilla extract. Add the honey mixture to the seed-and-fruit mixture, and stir well to combine.

Transfer the ingredients and bake.
Use a rubber spatula to scrape the mixture into the prepared baking dish, using the broad side of the spatula to press everything into an even layer. Bake until golden around the edges, 20 to 25 minutes. Transfer the baking dish to a wire cooling rack and let cool until firm, about 30 minutes.

Serve.
Use the parchment tabs to lift the seeded block out of the baking dish—if it starts to crumble, let it cool longer. Using a sharp knife, cut 16 bars. Eat the fruit-seed-nut bars at room temperature. Store any leftovers in a sealed container at room temperature for up to 5 days.

creamy blueberry bliss

PREP TIME
5 minutes

COOK TIME
none

SERVES
4

TOOLS / EQUIPMENT

Blender
Rubber spatula

1 ½ cups nonfat Greek yogurt

2 cups frozen blueberries

1 banana, cut into chunks,
or 2 tablespoons honey

3 tablespoons flax meal

¼ cup almond milk or whole milk

Ice, as desired

Purée the ingredients:
Spoon the yogurt into the blender, followed by the berries, banana, and flax meal. Purée until smooth, adding milk to thin the consistency slightly and ice as desired to keep it slushy. Stop the blender to scrape the sides down as needed.

Serve.
Pour into glasses and drink chilled.

TRY INSTEAD Consider adding a tablespoon of peanut butter for a PB&J theme. Swap blueberries for frozen strawberries and mango for a tropical vibe, or add raspberries and blackberries to the mix to make it extra berry.

fruity-nutty breakfast bowl

PREP TIME
10 minutes

COOK TIME
none

SERVES

4

**TOOLS /
EQUIPMENT**

Toaster oven

2 cups Greek yogurt

4 tablespoons flax meal

2 tablespoons chia seeds

4 tablespoons peanut butter

3 cups fresh fruit, such as pomegranate seeds, blueberries, raspberries, or chopped apples, persimmon, or pears

½ cup unsweetened coconut flakes, toasted

2 tablespoons nuts, toasted and coarsely chopped, such as almonds or pistachios (see Colorful Crunch Salad recipe, page 122)

Assemble the breakfast bowls and serve.
Stir the yogurt until creamy. Divide the yogurt evenly into bowls. Sprinkle the flax meal and chia seeds evenly into each. Spoon the peanut butter on top, then the fruit. Scatter the toasted coconut and chopped nuts to finish each bowl, and eat immediately.

HELPFUL HINT For easy toasted coconut, arrange the flakes in a single layer on a small piece of parchment on the toaster oven tray. Once coconut is golden, carefully lift parchment from the tray and sprinkle directly onto the bowls. No fussing or cleanup required!

ginger-lemon green juice

PREP TIME
10 minutes

COOK TIME
none

SERVES
4

**TOOLS /
EQUIPMENT**

Vegetable peeler

Blender

1 (2-inch) piece fresh ginger, peeled and cut into chunks

4 green apples, peeled and cored

2 lemons, peeled, seeds removed

1 orange, peeled, seeds removed

2 stalks lacinato kale, stems removed and coarsely chopped

2 sprigs fresh parsley, leaves only

1 ½ cups ice water

Purée the ingredients:

In a blender, purée the ginger and apples with the lemons and the orange, followed by the kale and parsley. Stop the blender to scrape the sides down as needed. If you prefer a thinner consistency, drizzle ice water through the feeder cap as the motor runs, stopping every few seconds to check the consistency.

Serve.

Pour into glasses and drink at once.

PRO TIP It's best to drink these juices right away. The purées themselves will keep for a day in the refrigerator without losing their vitamin potency, but they will oxidize, losing their bright color.

Perfect Hummus (page 98)

4

snacks & small bites

mini quiches

PREP TIME
10 minutes

COOK TIME
15 minutes

TOTAL TIME
30 minutes

MAKES
24
QUICHES

TOOLS / EQUIPMENT

Mini muffin tin
Medium bowl
Whisk
Baking sheet
Measuring cup

Butter, for greasing

4 whole eggs

1 egg yolk

⅓ cup heavy cream

¼ teaspoon freshly grated nutmeg

Pinch ground cayenne pepper

½ teaspoon kosher salt (if you choose bacon, ham, or smoked fish as your "delicious addition," reduce to a pinch of salt instead)

½ teaspoon freshly ground black pepper

¾ cup shredded Gruyère cheese, divided

Preheat the oven to 375°F.

Grease a 24-cup mini muffin tin.

Mix the ingredients.
In a medium bowl, whisk together the eggs, yolk, cream, nutmeg, cayenne, salt, and pepper until frothy. Stir in ½ cup of shredded cheese.

Add the quiche mixture to the pan.
Place the prepared muffin pan on a baking sheet to catch any drips. If you chose any delicious additions, add a teaspoonful to each cup. Transfer the egg mixture by ladling it into a measuring cup, and from there, pour the egg mixture into each cup, filling to just below the rim. The measuring cup's pour spout makes this a no-mess operation! Top the egg mixture with the remaining ¼ cup of shredded cheese, adding a small pinch to each quiche.

delicious additions

Steamed broccoli florets or chopped asparagus

Diced red bell pepper or chopped tomatoes

Sautéed sliced mushrooms

Sautéed spinach

Sautéed onions or shallots

Finely chopped chives or scallions

Bacon, cooked and crumbled, or ham

Smoked whitefish or salmon

Cook the quiches.

Bake until the tops are puffed and golden, 10 to 15 minutes. Let them cool for about 5 minutes.

Serve.

Invert the tin over the baking sheet to pop out the quiches. Arrange them on a platter or individual plates, and serve.

 TRY INSTEAD Feel free to use a different cheese: grated Comté, Swiss, or sharp Cheddar.

DID YOU KNOW? You can freeze extras after they have cooled completely on a small plate or tray. Once they are frozen (about 30 to 45 minutes), seal them in a freezer-safe container or bag. From there, they're good for up to two months! To reheat them, warm them in a 375°F oven for 8 to 10 minutes.

mighty meatballs

PREP TIME
20 minutes

COOK TIME
15 minutes

SERVES
4

**TOOLS /
EQUIPMENT**
Box grater
Fine grater
Small bowl
Medium bowl
Aluminum foil
Baking sheet

2 tablespoons buttermilk

¼ cup fresh bread crumbs

12 ounces ground beef

½ cup grated Parmesan cheese

2 pieces bacon, finely chopped

Pinch freshly grated nutmeg

1 egg

⅓ cup chopped fresh parsley

2 garlic cloves, grated

2 tablespoons olive oil

¼ teaspoon Kosher salt

¼ teaspoon freshly ground
black pepper

Mix the ingredients.

In a small bowl, add the buttermilk to the bread crumbs, and allow the crumbs to absorb the milk, 5 to 7 minutes. Meanwhile, put the ground beef in a medium bowl. Add the cheese, bacon, nutmeg, milk-soaked bread crumbs, egg, parsley, garlic, and olive oil to the meat, and sprinkle with salt and pepper. Overworking the mixture will produce tough, chewy meatballs, so mix everything just until combined.

Form the meat into balls.

Use 2 teaspoons to form the meat mixture into bite-size balls. Use the spoons to place them onto an aluminum-foil-lined baking sheet so that the heat of your hands doesn't warm them prior to cooking. Pre-heat the broiler with a rack in the topmost position.

Cook the meatballs.

Broil the meatballs until browned on top, checking them at about 5 minutes. Lower the heat to 350°F, and bake until tender and fully cooked, about 10 minutes.

Serve.

Serve warm on a serving platter or plates.

ricotta-jam toast

PREP TIME
5 minutes
plus 30 minutes
to warm

COOK TIME
5 minutes

SERVES
4

TOOLS /
EQUIPMENT
Zester
Toaster oven

2 to 4 tablespoons preserves of your choice—raspberry, blueberry, blackberry, or red currant

4 slices whole-grain, sourdough, or seeded bread

1 cup whole-milk ricotta cheese, well-stirred

Zest of 1 lemon

Prepare the preserves.
Let the preserves come to room temperature if you brought a jar from the refrigerator, about 30 minutes.

Assemble the toasts.
Toast the bread until golden and crispy at the edges, about 5 minutes. Spread the ricotta onto the toasts. Add a spoonful—or more, to your taste—of the preserves, and garnish with the lemon zest.

Serve.
These toasts are tasty served warm or at room temperature.

TRY INSTEAD Replace the lemon zest with freshly ground black pepper along with marmalade, applesauce, or persimmon preserves. Crumble a pinch of pink peppercorns over strawberry, fig, or apricot preserves.

from-scratch pizza

PREP TIME
20 minutes
plus 3–24 hours
to rest and rise

COOK TIME
10 minutes

SERVES
4

**TOOLS /
EQUIPMENT**

Fine grater

Large bowl

Small bowl

Pizza stone

Baking sheet

Tea towel

Parchment paper

Metal spatulas

1 cup plus 2 tablespoons all-purpose flour, plus extra for dusting

1 teaspoon kosher salt

1 cup water, mildly warm

¾ teaspoon active dry yeast

1 teaspoon olive oil

1 cup fresh mozzarella, torn

6 slices prosciutto, torn (optional)

½ cup Parmigiano-Reggiano, finely shredded

Flake salt, such as Maldon

Olive oil

2 to 3 cups fresh arugula, rinsed and patted dry

1 lemon, halved

Combine the dry ingredients.
In a large bowl, use a fork to stir the flour and salt together well.

Mix the yeast and knead the dough.
In a small bowl, stir the water and yeast together, add the olive oil, and stir again. Add this mixture to the flour mixture, and knead with your hands until well combined, about 3 minutes. Let the dough rest for 15 minutes.

Knead it again.
Knead the rested dough for 3 more minutes. Bring it out onto a heavily floured work surface, cut it in half, and use the outer edge of your palms to shape each into a ball. Cover the dough with a damp tea towel. Let rest and rise for 3 to 4 hours at room temperature, or 8 to 24 hours in the refrigerator.

Heat the pizza stone.
Place the pizza stone on the middle rack in your oven and preheat it to its highest setting for at least 1 hour.

Stretch the dough.
Place a dough ball on a well-floured surface, and use your fingertips, all together, to indent half an inch from the edge to make a border all the way around. Lift the dough and stretch it across your knuckles, pulling the thick areas thinner. Then lay it down and gently pull with your fingers to shape and stretch it farther as needed, until it is 12 inches wide. ❯❯

from-scratch pizza, continued

TROUBLESHOOTING To make this pizza, stretch your dough until it's pretty thin for a crispier pizza crust. There's a fine line between stretching and poking a hole, so pay attention to the thinning parts, and lay the dough down at any point if it becomes too fragile. Be patient; even if you "mess it up," the results will still taste delicious.

HELPFUL HINT Dough can be made three days in advance and should be made one day before making this recipe. If you refrigerated the dough, remove it 30 to 45 minutes before you shape it for the pizza.

Add the toppings.
Lay the stretched dough on a sheet of parchment paper laid on a well-floured overturned baking sheet and top the dough inside the border with the torn mozzarella and prosciutto, the shredded Parm, a pinch of salt, and a drizzle of olive oil.

Bake the pizza.
Use a quick, firm sliding motion to transfer the parchment and pizza to the pizza stone in the hot oven. Bake until the crust is golden and the cheese bubbles, about 10 minutes.

Dress the greens.
While the pizza cooks, transfer the arugula to a large bowl. Squeeze the lemon halves over the greens, cupping a hand underneath to catch any seeds, and toss to combine.

Serve.
Remove the pizza by lifting it from the parchment edges, then transfer the pizza with two spatulas to a cutting surface or platter. Top with the lemon-dressed greens, add another scatter of salt, cut into wedges, and eat at once. Repeat stretching and topping the second pizza, and cook it while you munch on the first.

potato-gruyère tart

PREP TIME
15 minutes
plus 10 minutes
to chill

COOK TIME
30 minutes

SERVES
4–6

**TOOLS /
EQUIPMENT**
Vegetable peeler
Box grater
Rolling pin
Baking sheet
Parchment paper
Paring knife
Large bowl

All-purpose flour, for dusting

1 package puff pastry, such as Dufour brand, thawed in the refrigerator

4 waxy potatoes, such as Yukon gold, peeled and sliced into ¼-inch-thick rounds

1 small onion, halved and sliced thin

1 to 2 tablespoons olive oil

3 to 5 fresh thyme sprigs, leaves only

Sea salt

Freshly ground black pepper

¾ cup Gruyère cheese, grated

Handful of fresh chives, minced, or arugula (optional)

Preheat the oven to 400°F.

Prepare the dough.
On a lightly floured work surface, unfold the dough and roll it out into a large rectangle about ⅛ inch thick. Arrange on a baking sheet lined with parchment paper, and prick the dough all over with a fork—this will ensure the dough doesn't swell up as it bakes. With a paring knife, make a border by gently scoring the dough along all four sides ¼ inch from the edge.

Chill the dough.
Refrigerate the dough for 10 minutes.

Prepare the toppings.
In a large bowl, toss the potatoes and onion in olive oil with the thyme leaves, and season with salt and pepper.

Assemble the tart.
Remove the baking sheet with dough from the refrigerator. Inside its border, sprinkle the grated cheese, then arrange the potato mixture on top. Season with salt and pepper.

Bake the tart.
Bake for 20 to 30 minutes, or until the potatoes are golden brown and cooked through.

Serve.
Cut into slices and enjoy! For added color and flavor, try garnishing the cooked tart with freshly snipped chives or fresh arugula.

moroccan pickled carrots

PREP TIME
10 minutes

COOK TIME
5 minutes

MAKES

1

PINT

**TOOLS /
EQUIPMENT**

Vegetable peeler

Mason jar with lid

Small saucepan

Whisk

Peel of 1 organic lemon, pith shaved off

2 dried chile peppers

2 garlic cloves

1 bay leaf

1 pound carrots, peeled and cut into
3- to 4-inch spears

½ teaspoon whole cumin seeds

1 teaspoon mustard seeds

Pinch black peppercorns

½ cup white or apple cider vinegar

⅓ cup filtered water

1 teaspoon honey

½ teaspoon kosher salt

Fill the jar.
Put the lemon peel, chiles, garlic, and bay leaf in the jar. Gently place it on its side, and pack the carrots in as tightly as they'll fit, tucking in the spices as you go.

Make the pickling liquid.
Turn the jar upright, and top with the cumin, mustard seeds, and peppercorns. In a small saucepan, heat the vinegar, water, honey, and salt until they dissolve, about 5 minutes, whisking the ingredients together to help speed the process.

Pickle the carrots.
Carefully pour the hot liquid into the jar over the carrot spears. The carrots should be completely covered by the liquid. Allow the liquid to cool to room temperature before sealing. Refrigerate for at least 1 week to allow the seasonings to take effect. Pickled carrots keep refrigerated for up to 1 month.

easy tzatziki

PREP TIME
15 minutes
plus 20 minutes
to drain

COOK TIME
none

MAKES

2½
CUPS

**TOOLS /
EQUIPMENT**

Fine grater
Colander
Large bowl

5 Persian cucumbers (or half an English cucumber), scrubbed and diced

1 teaspoon kosher salt

2 cups Greek yogurt

2 garlic cloves, finely grated

3 tablespoons fresh dill, chopped

1 tablespoon red wine vinegar

1 tablespoon olive oil

Freshly ground black pepper

Prep the cucumbers.
In a colander in the sink, sprinkle salt over the cucumbers, toss to combine, and let them sit for 20 minutes or so to drain their juices.

Release excess liquid.
Press the cucumbers to release any excess liquid, and transfer them to a large bowl.

Make the tzatziki.
Add the yogurt, garlic, dill, vinegar, and olive oil to the cucumbers, season with pepper, stir well to incorporate, and taste. Adjust to your liking, transfer to a sealed container, and refrigerate until ready to use. The dip keeps for 2 weeks.

DID YOU KNOW? Tzatziki can be made three days in advance and goes great with smoked fish, on toast, on grilled meats, swapped for salad dressing, and so much more.

FOOD FACT If your cucumbers are not organic, peel them first, as much of the pesticide residue is concentrated in the skin.

crispy fish sticks

PREP TIME
10 minutes

COOK TIME
15 minutes

SERVES
4

**TOOLS /
EQUIPMENT**
Zester
Citrus reamer
Baking sheet
2 shallow dishes
Whisk
Metal spatula

Olive oil, for greasing

1 pound flounder or cod fillets, cut into 1-inch strips

Flake salt, such as Maldon

Freshly ground black pepper

1 egg, beaten

Zest and juice of half a lemon

1 cup panko bread crumbs

1 tablespoon Old Bay or Italian seasoning

Tartar sauce, for serving

Lemon wedges, for serving

Preheat the oven to 425°F.

Prep the fish.
Lightly grease a baking sheet with olive oil. Pat the fish strips dry with paper towels and discard. Season the fish with salt and pepper, and set aside.

Prepare the egg mixture and breading.
In a shallow dish, whisk together the egg, lemon zest, and juice. In another shallow dish, stir the bread crumbs, Old Bay seasoning, and black pepper with a fork to combine.

Bread the fillets.
Dip the fish first in the egg mixture, letting any excess drip off, then press into the bread crumb mixture to adhere. Arrange the fish sticks in a single layer on the baking sheet, more toward the edges of the pan for better browning.

Bake the fish sticks.
Bake in the oven for 10 to 15 minutes, or until golden and the fish flakes easily with a fork, turning the pan halfway through for even baking.

Serve.
Use a spatula to transfer the fish sticks to a serving dish, and serve alongside tartar sauce and lemon wedges.

perfect hummus

PREP TIME
20 minutes
plus 8 hours to
soak and
10 minutes to sit

COOK TIME
1 hour

MAKES

4

CUPS

**TOOLS /
EQUIPMENT**

Citrus reamer

Mortar and pestle

Medium bowl

Colander

Large saucepan

Food processor

Rubber spatula

1 cup dried chickpeas

2 teaspoons baking soda, divided

4 garlic cloves

½ cup freshly squeezed lemon juice

1 teaspoon kosher salt, plus more
to season

¾ cup tahini

3 teaspoons cumin, toasted and ground

¼ cup ice water

Extra-virgin olive oil, for drizzling

Soak the chickpeas overnight.

In a medium bowl, cover the chickpeas and
1 teaspoon of baking soda with cold water by
2 inches. Cover with a pan lid, and let sit 8 hours
to overnight at room temperature, allowing
chickpeas to rehydrate. Drain and rinse.

Cook the chickpeas.

In a large saucepan over high heat, cover the
soaked chickpeas and remaining teaspoon of
baking soda with water by at least 2 inches. Bring to
a boil, skimming foam from the surface as needed.
Reduce the heat to medium-low, place pan lid to
mostly cover, and simmer until the chickpeas are
tender and falling apart, about 45 minutes to an
hour. Drain and set aside.

Process the mixture.

In a food processor, pulse the garlic, lemon juice,
and salt until the mixture becomes a coarse paste.

Add the tahini and water.

Add the tahini to the garlic mixture, and pulse to
combine. With the motor running, add the ice water
1 tablespoon at a time and pulse until the mixture is
smooth, pale, and thick. The initial shock of the cold
water may make the mixture seize up at first.

delicious additions

Smoked paprika

Chopped fresh parsley

Ground sumac

Roasted red peppers

Aleppo pepper

Lemon zest

Add the chickpeas and spices.

Add the chickpeas and cumin to the mixture, and pulse until the hummus is very smooth, about 3 minutes, stopping as needed to scrape down the sides. Add more ice water if you want a thinner consistency. Taste and season with more salt, cumin, and/or lemon juice if needed. Let the hummus sit for 20 minutes to allow flavors to meld, up to overnight.

Serve.

Transfer the hummus to a shallow dish and swirl to make a well in the center of it. Drizzle with olive oil, and serve with veggie spears, pita bread, chips, grilled meats, on toast—really, just about anything.

HELPFUL HINT In warmer weather, soak chickpeas overnight in the fridge to reduce the risk of bacteria. Give them a quick rinse, cook as instructed, and you're good to go!

pita veggie pockets

PREP TIME
10 minutes

COOK TIME
3 minutes

SERVES
4

**TOOLS /
EQUIPMENT**

Toaster oven

2 whole grain pita pockets, sliced in half

CREAMY—CHOOSE 1

1 cup Perfect Hummus (page 98), black bean dip, avocado, scrambled eggs, Labneh, or Greek yogurt

CRUNCHY—CHOOSE 3

2 carrots, cut into disks or matchsticks

2 Persian cucumbers, chopped

2 radishes, sliced thin

1 colorful bell pepper, diced

Handful arugula, baby spinach, or lettuce

1/3 cup almonds, toasted and slivered

BRIGHT AND ZINGY—CHOOSE 2 TO 3

Handful fresh parsley, dill, or mint

Handful olives

1 tablespoon pickled onions

1/3 cup crumbled feta cheese or shaved Parmesan

Toast the pockets.
Toast the pita pockets in the toaster oven—it may take two rounds of toasting depending on the size of your toaster oven.

Assemble the pockets.
Spread or spoon your creamy element onto the insides of each pita pocket. Divide the crunchy ingredients evenly among the pockets, pressing in the ends to open the pocket up like a purse and layering the fillings in. Sprinkle the bright and zingy elements to top or tuck them in between the crunchy and creamy layers.

Serve.
Eat immediately or within 24 hours for best result. Refrigerate the sandwiches in a sealable bag or container if you make them more than 4 hours in advance of when you plan to eat them.

DID YOU KNOW? Labneh is a custard-like cheese most similar to Greek yogurt. It is prized for its rich texture and bright tanginess. You can find it at Middle Eastern grocers, specialty shops, and online.

no-nonsense guacamole

PREP TIME
10 minutes

COOK TIME
3 minutes

SERVES
4

TOOLS / EQUIPMENT
Fine grater
Citrus reamer
Small skillet
Mortar and pestle
Medium bowl
Wooden spoon

2 teaspoons cumin seeds

4 avocados, halved and pitted

1 garlic clove, finely grated

½ teaspoon chili powder

Juice of 3 limes

⅓ cup chopped fresh cilantro

Flake salt, such as Maldon

Tortilla chips, for serving

Toast the spice.
In a small dry skillet over medium heat, toast the cumin until fragrant, about 3 minutes. Transfer to a mortar and pestle, and grind into a powder.

Combine the ingredients.
Scoop the avocado flesh into a medium bowl, and coarsely mash with a fork. Add the garlic, chili powder, lime juice, and cilantro, season with salt, and stir to combine. Taste and adjust seasoning as needed.

Serve.
Serve the guacamole with tortilla chips, on tacos, or with eggs, grilled meats and seafood, and more. To store any leftovers, squeeze a little lime or lemon juice onto the guacamole, stir to combine, and immediately seal in an airtight container so it does not oxidize. Keeps for up to 2 days in the refrigerator.

anything quesadillas

PREP TIME
5 minutes

COOK TIME
10 minutes

SERVES
4

**TOOLS/
EQUIPMENT**

Box grater

Large skillet

Metal spatula

6 (10-inch) flour tortillas

Olive oil, for pan frying

Kosher salt

Freshly ground black pepper

**AS A GENERAL RULE, USE THIS
RATIO, PER QUESADILLA:**

3 to 4 tablespoons condiments
(such as herbs, mustard, or onions)

⅓ cup main ingredient (such as sliced
meat, mashed squash, roasted veggies)

⅔ cup grated cheese of your choice

Prep the tortilla.

Generously spread one tortilla with any sauce-like,
condiment. It may be cream cheese to go with the
smoked salmon, mustard to go with the corned
beef, etc. Set it aside; this will be the tortilla to sandwich the layers once they are in the pan.

Layer the elements.

Set a large skillet over medium heat. When the pan
is hot, drizzle with oil and swirl to coat. Place a tortilla into the skillet, and spoon your main ingredient
item onto it, spreading it all the way to the edge.

Sandwich the quesadilla, and cook.

Sprinkle the cheese over, all the way to the edge. If
you have any herbs, add them to top the cheese.
Lay the prepped tortilla facedown onto the rest,
pressing down on it evenly with a metal spatula to
compress the layers. Cover the pan with a lid, and if
needed, lower the heat slightly so that you do not
burn the bottom tortilla.

Cook and flip the quesadilla.

Cook covered for 2 to 3 minutes, or long enough
for the cheese to begin melting. This is the "glue" to
hold the fillings together when you flip the tortilla.
In one swift move, use the spatula to flip the quesadilla over. You may use another spatula or serving
spoon to steady the top side as you prepare to flip.
This requires some coordination but helps guarantee that the fillings stay put.

delicious combinations

Any of these flavor combos are great, listed here in the order of main ingredient, condiment, cheese:

BLT with sharp Cheddar or blue cheese

Tuna melt with pepper Jack

Corned beef, sauerkraut, and mustard with Swiss

Ham, honey mustard, and Swiss cheese

Sage-roasted and mashed sweet potato or butternut squash with Parmesan or blue cheese

Sliced tomatoes, chives, and mayo with dill Havarti

Turkey, roasted peppers, and mashed avocado with Gouda

Smoked salmon, dill, cucumbers, and cream cheese

Cooked steak, peppers, and onions with Muenster

Roasted zucchini or mushrooms, parsley, olives, and mozzarella

Refried beans, lime, cilantro, and queso fresco

Continue cooking.

Once the quesadilla is flipped, add a drizzle of olive oil to the pan as needed. Swirl to coat and cook for another 2 minutes, using the spatula to compress the layers together, until the cheese is well-melted and the quesadilla is brown and crispy.

Serve.

Transfer the quesadilla to a cutting board, and slice into wedges. Allow to cool for at least 2 minutes so the hot cheese does not burn you. Serve with fresh herbs, if desired.

GET CREATIVE

As you explore the world of food, you'll discover all kinds of flavor combos. Get creative and adapt your favorites here, with the added yum of melty, gooey cheese, just like the name "queso" in quesadillas says.

gazpacho gulps

PREP TIME
10 minutes plus
3 hours to chill

COOK TIME
none

SERVES
4

**TOOLS /
EQUIPMENT**
Blender
Rubber spatula

2 pounds tomatoes, cored and cut
into chunks

1 cubanelle pepper, cored, seeded, and
cut into chunks

1 cucumber, peeled and cut into chunks

1 small white or red onion, cut
into chunks

1 or 2 garlic cloves, halved

1 teaspoon kosher salt

1 teaspoon freshly ground
black pepper

2 teaspoons sherry vinegar, plus more
to taste

½ cup olive oil, plus more for drizzling

Purée the vegetables.
In a blender, blend the tomatoes, pepper, cucumber, onion, and garlic at high speed until very smooth, about 2 minutes, stopping periodically to scrape down the sides with a rubber spatula. Season with salt and pepper.

Add the remaining ingredients.
With the motor running, add the vinegar and slowly drizzle in the olive oil through the feeder cap. The mixture will turn bright orange or pinkish. Blending as you add the oil will emulsify the mixture, making it creamy.

Serve.
Transfer the gazpacho to a glass pitcher and refrigerate for 3 hours, or until well chilled. Before serving, season with additional salt and vinegar to taste. Serve in small glasses with a drizzle of olive oil—preferably sipped in the sun.

> HELPFUL HINT Leftover gazpacho will last up to five days, kept refrigerated and covered. Give leftovers a good stir just before serving.

crispy sesame seaweed

PREP TIME
5 minutes
plus 15 minutes
to marinate

COOK TIME
5 minutes

MAKES
16
SHEETS

**TOOLS/
EQUIPMENT**
Small bowl
Parchment paper
Pastry brush
Rubber band
Large cast-
iron skillet
Tongs
Metal spatula

2 tablespoons safflower or
grapeseed oil

2 tablespoons sesame oil

Kosher salt

16 sheets nori seaweed

Prepare the marinade.
In a small bowl, stir the safflower and sesame oils to combine.

Dress the seaweed.
Set a sheet of nori, shiny-side up, on a piece of parchment large enough to extend a couple inches beyond the nori in all directions. Brush a light layer of oil onto it, and lightly sprinkle with salt. Repeat with the remaining seaweed sheets as you stack them, shiny-side up, on top of each other on the parchment.

Marinate the seaweed.
Roll the nori stack in the parchment, and fasten it with a rubber band, helping to keep the parchment rolled around the seaweed as it marinates. Let the rolled bundle sit for at least 15 minutes before toasting.

Crisp the seaweed.
Place a large cast-iron skillet over medium heat. Once hot, place one nori sheet from the bundle in the pan shiny-side up, and pressing on it with the back of a spatula, toast for 15 seconds, or until it begins to get crispy and turn a brighter green. Add another piece of seaweed on top of the first, rough side facing up. Use tongs to flip the stack over, and add another nori sheet rough-side up. Toast for about 15 seconds again. Repeat this process until all 16 sheets have been added, flipping and toasting until they become crispy and green.

Serve.

When all the sheets have been crisped, you can use kitchen shears to cut the nori into smaller rectangles or other shapes, as you like. Keep leftovers in a resealable bag or an airtight container, at room temperature, and use within 10 days.

> HELPFUL HINT The oil mixture and salt will distribute evenly on both sides of the seaweed sheets, since they were rolled in a stack together. For best results, the key in this preparation is to keep the rough side facing out as you toast.

Delicious Delicata Rings (page 131)

5

salads & veggies

savory cabbage slaw

PREP TIME
15 minutes
plus 20 minutes
to sit

COOK TIME
none

SERVES
4

**TOOLS /
EQUIPMENT**

Citrus reamer

Small bowl

Whisk

Large bowl

4 tablespoons olive oil

3 tablespoons fish sauce

1 tablespoon sherry vinegar

Juice of 1 lime

1 teaspoon brown sugar

Flake salt, such as Maldon

½ head red cabbage

½ head green cabbage

Freshly ground black pepper

Make the dressing.

In a small bowl, combine the olive oil, fish sauce, vinegar, lime juice, sugar, and a small pinch of salt, whisking vigorously to dissolve the sugar. Taste, adjust seasoning as needed, and set aside.

Make the slaw.

With the flat side of the cabbage flush against your cutting board, use a very sharp knife to slice the cabbage very thinly and transfer to a large bowl. Use two forks to toss half the dressing in with the cabbage mix. Add the remainder, and toss again to coat. Season with pepper.

Serve.

The slaw is best once the acids in the dressing soften the crunchy cabbage slightly, at least 20 minutes. Before serving, toss the slaw to reincorporate the dressing accumulated at the bottom of the bowl, then pile the slaw onto sandwiches or serve as a super-flavorful, crunchy side. Keeps in the refrigerator, covered, for 1 week.

TRY INSTEAD The addition of a couple julienned carrots and a thinly sliced, seeded jalapeño make this zippy slaw even more festive.

asian cucumber salad

PREP TIME
10 minutes
plus 10 minutes
to sit

COOK TIME
3
minutes

SERVES
4

**TOOLS /
EQUIPMENT**

Medium bowl

Whisk

Small skillet

3 tablespoons rice wine vinegar

1 tablespoon toasted sesame oil

1 tablespoon soy sauce

½ teaspoon sugar

4 cups Persian, hothouse, or other
thin-skinned cucumbers, scrubbed
and chopped

2 scallions, ends trimmed and sliced
thin on a diagonal

⅓ cup chopped fresh cilantro

Pinch flake salt, such as Maldon

1 tablespoon sesame seeds

delicious additions

Minced pickled or fresh ginger
Minced garlic
Red pepper flakes
Bonito flakes

Make the dressing.
In a medium bowl, whisk to combine the rice wine
vinegar, sesame oil, soy sauce, and sugar, dissolving
the sugar.

Compose the salad.
Add the cucumbers, scallions, cilantro, and salt, and
toss to coat well. Taste and adjust seasoning as necessary. Allow the salad to sit for at least 10 minutes
for the flavors to meld.

Toast the seeds.
In a small dry skillet over medium heat, toast the
sesame seeds until golden, about 3 minutes.

Serve.
Serve chilled with the toasted sesame seeds sprinkled on top. Pairs well with grilled meats, seared fish
or shrimp, brown rice, or broiled, marinated tofu.

PRO TIP Think about how you'll use the
cucumber salad before you chop. For
a stand-alone salad, thin circle slices have a
delicate presentation. Paired with grilled meat
or fish, diced cucumber offers a crunchy
contrast to the juicy main attraction.

summery corn and watermelon salad

PREP TIME
15 minutes

COOK TIME
none

SERVES
4

TOOLS / EQUIPMENT

Zester

5 fresh basil leaves

½ small watermelon, seeded, rind removed, cut into 1-inch cubes

2 ears fresh sweet corn, cooked and cut off cob

1 teaspoon ground sumac

¼ teaspoon ground cayenne

Zest of ½ lemon

Flake salt, such as Maldon

Assemble the salad.
Transfer the cubed watermelon and any accumulated juices to a serving platter. Add the corn cut off the cobs (it is okay if there are rows of corn left intact; that is part of the fun). Sprinkle the sumac and cayenne over the mixture, followed by the lemon zest.

Cut the basil into a chiffonade.
Do this immediately prior to serving the salad, as the edges of the basil will darken from being cut (known as oxidation). Stack the basil leaves on top of each other, and roll into a tight bundle. Slice your knife across the roll, creating very thin strips (called chiffonade). Fluff the chiffonade to separate the strips, and scatter onto the salad.

Serve.
Season with salt, and serve immediately.

FOOD FACT The fresher corn is, the juicier, more tender, and sweeter its kernels. To tell when a watermelon is its ripest, look for a light spot on one side of the skin: This means it was allowed to ripen on the vine rather than being harvested prematurely.

panzanella salad

PREP TIME
15 minutes

COOK TIME
10 minutes

SERVES
4

TOOLS /
EQUIPMENT

Bread knife

Baking sheet

Small bowl

Whisk

1 loaf crusty bread, torn into bite-size chunks and left to dry out on a baking sheet for 1 to 2 days

2 tablespoons olive oil, plus extra for soaking, drizzling, and frying

Flake salt, such as Maldon

Freshly ground black pepper

5 large heirloom tomatoes, cut into wedges

1 ½ cups Sun Gold tomatoes, halved

2 cups fresh basil leaves, rinsed and patted dry

4 chives, finely chopped

2 teaspoons red wine vinegar

TRY INSTEAD Substitute shallots cut into wedges and slowly sautéed until soft and translucent, or thinly sliced raw or pickled red onion for the chives.

Preheat the oven to 425°F.

Toast the bread.

Arrange the bread on a baking sheet, and drizzle with olive oil, and season with salt and pepper. Toast the bread in the oven until golden and crisp on the edges, turning once halfway through as needed, about 8 minutes total.

Assemble the salad.

Arrange the tomatoes on a serving platter, alternating shapes and colors. Add the basil, and nestle the crispy bread into the mixture, then scatter the chives all around.

Make the dressing.

In a small bowl, whisk the olive oil and red wine vinegar to combine.

Serve.

Drizzle the dressing over the salad, saving some for at the table, season with salt and pepper, and dig in. You just made an edible work of art!

DID YOU KNOW? This salad is best made when tomatoes are in season during summertime. Look for heirlooms that are heavy, as they'll be bursting with juice and flavor. Different heirloom tomatoes, such as Green Zebras, Cherokee Purples, Yellow Pineapples, or Brandywines add a rainbow of color to the panzanella, as well as subtly different flavors.

minty avocado-melon mix

PREP TIME
15 minutes

COOK TIME
10 minutes

SERVES
4

**TOOLS /
EQUIPMENT**

Citrus reamer

Small bowl

Small cast-
iron skillet

Metal spatula

Melon baller

⅓ cup plus 1 tablespoon
olive oil, divided

2 limes, one juiced and one cut into
wedges for serving

¼ cup chopped fresh mint

Sea salt

Freshly ground black pepper

1 (8-ounce) block Haloumi cheese,
sliced into ¼-inch slices

1 cantaloupe, halved and seeded

2 avocados, halved and pitted

HELPFUL HINT Set aside
any cantaloupe pieces
that are too small for use later,
served over yogurt or with
granola or for making into ice
pops. You can save any
leftover avocado for making
No-Nonsense Guacamole
(page 101).

Make the dressing.
In a small bowl, stir together ⅓ cup of olive oil with
the juice of 1 lime, mint, and salt and pepper to
taste. Set aside.

Fry the cheese.
In a small cast-iron skillet over medium-high heat,
heat the remaining 1 tablespoon of olive oil. Add
the cheese slices, and lower the heat to medium.
Moisture from the cheese can cause the oil to spat-
ter, so be careful as you lay them in. Sear the cheese
for a few minutes—you should hear them sizzle.
Flip to the second side when the first is caramelized
and browned. The second side takes only a couple
minutes. Transfer to a serving platter.

Prepare the melon.
Use a melon baller to make spheres from the cantaloupe's flesh, and then arrange them on the platter
beside the Haloumi.

Prepare the avocado.
Repeat the process with the avocados. Do this just
before serving time so that the avocado doesn't
oxidize, and squeeze a wedge or two of fresh lime
juice over the avocado spheres, tossing to coat.

Serve.
Layer the mixture of avocado and melon balls next
to the Haloumi, and spoon the chopped mint dressing over all. Serve with the remaining lime wedges,
and eat immediately.

salade niçoise

PREP TIME
10 minutes

COOK TIME
7 minutes

SERVES
4

**TOOLS /
EQUIPMENT**

Paring knife

Vegetable peeler

Small bowl

Whisk

Large saucepan

Large
slotted spoon

Large bowl

Colander

FOR THE DRESSING

½ cup olive oil

2 tablespoons white wine vinegar

1 teaspoon Dijon mustard

1 small shallot, minced

3 tablespoons finely chopped
fresh parsley

Kosher salt

Freshly ground black pepper

[INGREDIENT LIST CONTINUES ON NEXT PAGE]

To make the dressing.
In a small bowl, whisk to combine the olive oil, vinegar, mustard, shallot, and parsley. Season with salt and pepper, and set aside.

Boil the eggs.
In a saucepan large enough to fit the eggs in a single layer, add enough water to cover them by 1 inch, and bring the water to a boil. Use a large spoon to carefully lower refrigerator-cold eggs into the water, one at a time, and return to a simmer, adjusting heat as necessary. Simmer for 6 minutes for a liquid-gold yolk, 7 to 9 minutes for a custardy yolk. After your preferred cook time, use a slotted spoon to transfer the eggs to a large bowl filled with ice water.

Peel the eggs.
Once the eggs are cool enough to handle, tap them on the counter to crack the shells all over, and carefully peel them. Rinse each briefly under cold water to remove any stray shell bits, then quarter them.

Cut the potatoes.
Once they are cool enough to handle, slice potatoes into bite-sized wedges and set aside.

Cut the haricots verts.
Stack the haricots verts and slice them into bite-size pieces on a sharp diagonal.

FOR THE SALAD

4 eggs, cold

Ice water

5 potatoes, peeled and boiled until fork tender

2 handfuls very fresh haricots verts, scrubbed, stem ends trimmed

1 head romaine, Bibb lettuce, or arugula, leaves rinsed and patted dry

5 radishes, sliced into thin wedges

½ cup pitted Niçoise (or other oil-cured) olives

1 lemon, sliced into rounds

2 cans oil-packed tuna, drained

2 tablespoons finely chopped chives or thinly sliced red onion

1 tablespoon capers, rinsed

6 anchovies (optional)

delicious additions

Cooked artichoke hearts

Steamed asparagus

Cherry tomatoes or tomato wedges

Marinated beets

Assemble the salad and serve.

On a serving platter, arrange salad leaves to cover. Stack the quartered eggs, haricots verts, sliced radishes, olives, lemon wheels, and boiled potatoes into piles or rows, alongside the chunks of tuna. Scatter the chives and capers over everything, add the anchovies (if using) piled either in the center or laid out over the other elements, and spoon the dressing over all. Serve immediately.

HELPFUL HINT The vinaigrette, potatoes, and eggs can be prepared two days in advance. When thin green beans such as haricots verts are very fresh, they do not need to be cooked. Leaving them raw adds more crunchy nuance to the salad and saves on prep time.

DID YOU KNOW? Niçoise salad is a famous French composed salad that tradition-ally has tuna and anchovies on top of piles of colorful ingredients.

not-your-average caesar

PREP TIME
10 minutes
plus 30 minutes
to chill

COOK TIME
10 minutes

SERVES
4

**TOOLS /
EQUIPMENT**
Citrus reamer
Box grater
Blender
Rubber spatula
Mason jar with lid
Baking sheet
Large bowl

5 anchovies, plus extra for garnish

2 garlic cloves

2 tablespoons Dijon mustard

1 tablespoon freshly squeezed lemon juice

1 tablespoon white wine vinegar or champagne vinegar

1 large egg

¾ cup olive oil, plus additional oil for drizzling

¼ cup Parmigiano-Reggiano cheese, finely grated, plus more for serving

½ loaf crusty bread, 1 to 3 days old, diced or torn into bite-size pieces

2 heads romaine lettuce, root ends trimmed, quartered, and coarsely chopped

Pinch freshly ground black pepper

Preheat the oven to 400°F.

Make the dressing.
In a blender, blend the anchovies and garlic until they become a rough paste. Add the mustard, lemon juice, and vinegar, crack in the egg, and blend until the mixture is smooth and creamy. With the blender on, remove the feeder cap and gradually drizzle in the olive oil in a steady stream. Turn the blender off. Add the cheese, and blend again until all ingredients are well combined. Scrape the dressing into a mason jar with a rubber spatula, seal it, and refrigerate for 15 to 30 minutes, or until it thickens.

Make the croutons.
Meanwhile, on a baking sheet, spread the bread pieces in a single layer and drizzle with olive oil. Bake for 12 minutes, or until golden and crisp at the edges.

Assemble the salad.
In a large bowl, pour half the dressing over the chopped lettuce, and toss with a large fork and spoon. Add some of your croutons and toss a little more, so that some are coated in the dressing.

Serve.
Pile the salad into bowls, adding a few more croutons to each serving as you like and one or two anchovies to garnish. Drizzle on additional dressing to taste, grate more cheese on top, and finish with the pepper. The dressing will keep for up to 3 days, sealed in the refrigerator.

emerald salad with buttermilk dressing

PREP TIME
10 minutes

COOK TIME
none

SERVES
4

TOOLS / EQUIPMENT
Fine grater
Mason jar with lid

½ cup buttermilk

2 to 3 tablespoons sour cream

1 teaspoon Dijon mustard

1 tablespoon apple cider vinegar

2 tablespoons chopped fresh chives, tarragon, dill, or parsley, or a combination

1 garlic clove, finely grated

Few dashes hot sauce

¼ teaspoon freshly ground black pepper

Pinch flake salt, such as Maldon

3 heads lettuce (such as gem, Bibb, or butter), root ends trimmed and quartered lengthwise

Make the dressing.

In a mason jar with a lid, combine the buttermilk, sour cream, mustard, vinegar, chives, garlic, hot sauce, pepper, and salt. Close it tightly, then shake it like crazy. After 30 seconds to a minute of vigorous shaking, open the jar and taste, adjust the seasonings as needed, seal, and shake again.

Serve.

Divide the lettuce wedges and herbs evenly onto plates. Spoon the dressing directly from the mason jar onto the greens. Sprinkle salt and pepper to taste. Any remaining dressing will keep sealed, in the refrigerator, for up to 5 days. You'll want to use it on everything: roasted potatoes, carrot spears, roast chicken, and more!

FOOD FACT All that shaking emulsifies—or blends—the ingredients, suspending the water molecules inside the fat molecules. What results is a creamy, dreamy dressing.

grainy mustard-potato salad

PREP TIME
10 minutes

COOK TIME
10 minutes

SERVES
4

**TOOLS/
EQUIPMENT**
Large saucepan
Colander
Large bowl

6 medium Yukon gold potatoes, scrubbed and cut into chunky wedges

3 medium Red Bliss potatoes, scrubbed and cut into chunky wedges

4 to 5 tablespoons olive oil

2 tablespoons whole-grain mustard

1 tablespoon capers, well-rinsed and chopped

1 shallot, sliced thin

3 tablespoons dill, torn into small sprigs

Sea salt

Freshly ground black pepper

Boil the potatoes.
In a large saucepan, cover the potatoes with water and gently boil them for 8 to 10 minutes, until fork-tender. Drain the potatoes in a colander, and transfer to a large bowl.

Dress the potatoes.
In a large bowl, toss the olive oil, mustard, capers, and shallot to combine with the potatoes.

Serve.
Once the potato mixture has cooled to room temperature, add the dill sprigs, and toss again. Season to taste with salt and pepper. Enjoy warm, at room temperature, or chilled.

nutty parmesan-kale salad

PREP TIME
15 minutes

COOK TIME
10 minutes

SERVES
4

TOOLS / EQUIPMENT

Citrus reamer

Zester

Vegetable peeler

Large bowl

Baking sheet

Toaster oven

Small serving bowl

1 bunch lacinato kale, also known as Tuscan or dinosaur kale, rinsed, ends trimmed

Zest and juice of 1 lemon

2 tablespoons olive oil

Flake salt, such as Maldon

Freshly ground black pepper

1 cup hazelnuts

½ cup shaved Parmigiano-Reggiano

Chop the kale.
Gather the kale into a tight bunch or stack the leaves on top of each other, and slice into very thin strips, about ⅛ inch wide. Transfer to a large bowl.

Dress the salad.
Add the lemon zest and juice and the olive oil to the bowl, season with salt and pepper, and toss to combine. Taste and adjust seasoning, and set aside.

Prepare the nuts.
Toast the hazelnuts for 5 minutes or until fragrant. When cool enough to handle, gently rub off their skins. Arrange the nuts on a cutting board. Coarsely crush them by leaning your weight onto the side of a chef's knife placed on them. Transfer nuts to the toaster oven tray and toast again until golden, about 3 minutes more. Empty the nuts into a small serving bowl.

Serve.
At the table, scatter the hazelnuts and shaved Parm over the salad, and serve immediately.

> HELPFUL HINT Chopping and dressing the kale can be done a day in advance, giving time for the citrus to break down the leaves' sturdiness. If you do make it ahead, toss again before adding final toppings to redistribute the dressing.

colorful crunch salad

PREP TIME
15 minutes

COOK TIME
5 minutes

SERVES
4

**TOOLS /
EQUIPMENT**

Toaster oven

4 red, orange, and yellow bell peppers, cored and sliced into thin, bite-size strips

2 celery stalks, diced

1 handful green beans, ends trimmed, sliced into thin coins

¼ cup chopped fresh parsley

2 tablespoons capers, rinsed and chopped

2 tablespoons olive oil

2 teaspoons sherry or champagne vinegar

Freshly ground black pepper

⅓ cup slivered almonds

Toast the nuts.
Arrange almonds in a single layer on a toaster oven tray. Toast for 4 minutes, or until they become fragrant and their edges turn golden. You may agitate pan halfway through, circulating the almonds for even toasting. Transfer them to a small dish.

Assemble the salad.
Layer the peppers, celery, green beans, parsley, and capers onto a serving platter. Toss slightly to incorporate.

Serve.
Drizzle the salad with the olive oil and vinegar, season with pepper, and scatter the toasted almonds on top. Serve immediately.

egg salad and toast points

PREP TIME
10 minutes

COOK TIME
15 minutes

SERVES

4

TOOLS / EQUIPMENT

Citrus reamer

Large saucepan

Large bowl

Large slotted spoon

Toaster oven

Medium bowl

8 eggs

Ice water

4 slices crusty bread, such as sourdough or seeded wheat, crusts removed, and cut diagonally in half, into triangles

2 tablespoons mayonnaise

2 teaspoons Dijon mustard

1 teaspoon freshly squeezed lemon juice

1 celery stalk, finely chopped

1 tablespoon finely chopped cornichons

1 tablespoon finely chopped parsley

Sea salt

Freshly ground black pepper

Cook the eggs.

In a saucepan large enough for the eggs to sit in a single layer, bring to a boil enough water to submerge the eggs by at least 1 inch. Carefully lower the eggs into the water, return to a boil, and simmer for 10 minutes. Have a large bowl filled with ice water nearby.

Transfer and peel the eggs.

Use a slotted spoon to transfer the eggs to the water to chill them for peeling. Let the eggs sit in the ice bath until cool to the touch. Tap the eggshell on your work surface, turning it and cracking it throughout. Peel the shells and discard.

Toast the bread.

Toast the bread pieces in the toaster oven until golden and crisp. Transfer to individual plates or a serving dish.

Assemble the salad.

In a medium bowl, use a fork or potato masher to mash the hard-cooked eggs, combining them with the mayonnaise, mustard, and lemon juice. You may opt to keep the consistency chunky, or for a creamier consistency, mash until well combined.

DID YOU KNOW? If the eggs are very fresh, adding ¼ teaspoon kosher salt to the cooking water will make them easier to peel. Eggshells and other vegetable clippings make great nutrients for compost. Save them in a plastic bag in the refrigerator, and when it becomes full, empty it in a designated spot in your backyard to break down into the soil. There is a wealth of information in your local library or online about how to make proper compost, which is the best food for plants, flowers, and trees.

Finish assembling.
Add the celery, cornichons, and parsley, and season with salt and pepper. Stir gently to combine.

Serve.
Serve with the toast points chilled or at room temperature. Any leftovers will keep, sealed in the refrigerator, for up to 4 days.

roasted cauliflower with dipping sauce

PREP TIME
10 minutes

COOK TIME
55 minutes

SERVES
4

TOOLS / EQUIPMENT

Citrus reamer

Box grater

Dutch oven

Rubber spatula

Small bowl

Roasting pan

FOR THE CAULIFLOWER

1 ½ cups dry white wine or white wine vinegar

6 cups water

⅓ cup olive oil, plus more for serving

3 tablespoons kosher salt

3 tablespoons freshly squeezed lemon juice

2 tablespoons orange juice

2 tablespoons butter

1 tablespoon crushed red pepper flakes

Pinch black peppercorns

1 bay leaf

1 head cauliflower, stem trimmed

Flake salt, such as Maldon, for serving

[INGREDIENT LIST CONTINUES ON NEXT PAGE]

Poach the cauliflower.

In a Dutch oven or other heavy-bottomed pot over high heat, bring the wine, water, olive oil, kosher salt, lemon juice, orange juice, butter, red pepper flakes, peppercorns, and bay leaf to a boil. Add the cauliflower, then reduce the heat to simmer. Turn occasionally, using a pair of serving spoons to submerge each side in the poaching liquid, until a knife easily inserts into center, 15 to 20 minutes.

Preheat the oven to 475°F.

Make the dipping sauce.

In a small bowl, mix together the crème fraîche, Greek yogurt, cheese, and capers, and season with pepper. Set aside.

Roast the cauliflower.

Using tongs or the serving spoons, transfer cauliflower to a roasting pan. Roast, rotating the sheet if browning unevenly, until deep golden and crispy in parts, about 35 minutes.

FOR THE SAUCE

½ cup crème fraîche

3 tablespoons nonfat Greek yogurt

¼ cup finely shredded Parmigiano-Reggiano

3 teaspoons capers, rinsed and chopped

Freshly ground black pepper

Serve.

Bring the roasted cauliflower to the table, set on a trivet, and serve directly from the roasting pan with the dipping sauce—and a spoon to dispense it—alongside.

FOOD FACT Capers are the pickled flower buds of a shrub that grows in dry climates in the Mediterranean, and to harvest them, people pick them off the plant one by one. If you can find salt-packed rather than brined capers, they will keep in your pantry indefinitely and are more robust in flavor. Find them in specialty shops or online.

PRO TIP After cooking the cauliflower, the poaching liquid can be reserved and used again: to cook rice or quinoa, or as stock for soup.

honey-roasted carrots with rosemary

PREP TIME
10 minutes

COOK TIME
35 minutes

SERVES
4

TOOLS / EQUIPMENT
Small saucepan

Whisk

Baking sheet

Rubber spatula

2 tablespoons butter

2 tablespoons honey

Flake salt, such as Maldon

2 to 3 bunches small carrots, scrubbed and greens trimmed, halved lengthwise if thick

2 fresh rosemary sprigs, quills stripped from stems and coarsely chopped

Freshly ground black pepper

Preheat the oven to 425°F.

Prepare the glaze.
In a small saucepan over medium heat, melt the butter. Add the honey, and whisk to dissolve. Season with a pinch of salt, and set aside.

Toss the ingredients together.
On a baking sheet, drizzle the honey mixture over the carrots, toss to coat, and scatter the chopped rosemary on top. Season with salt and pepper.

Roast the carrots.
Bake for 30 to 35 minutes, or until the carrots are tender and caramelized in spots, rearranging them for even browning halfway through.

Serve.
Transfer to a serving platter or plates and eat warm.

PRO TIP While there's no need to peel the carrots in this recipe, you can save the peels and cut the ends from carrots, along with the ends, skins, and stems of onions, parsley, and celery, in a resealable bag kept in the freezer for making homemade stock. When the bag is full, you know it's time to make stock.

roasted brussels sprouts and shallots

PREP TIME
10 minutes

COOK TIME
30 minutes

SERVES
4

**TOOLS/
EQUIPMENT**

2 baking sheets

Tongs

1 ½ pounds Brussels sprouts, trimmed and halved

6 shallots, quartered

3 tablespoons olive oil

Sea salt

Freshly ground black pepper

1 lemon, cut into wedges, for serving

Arrange oven racks and preheat oven.
Place one oven rack in the top third of the oven and another in the bottom third, then preheat oven to 450°F.

Prep the veggie mixture.
On two baking sheets, toss the Brussels sprouts and shallots with the olive oil, placing most of the Brussels halves cut-side down. Season with salt and pepper.

Roast the vegetables.
Swap the pans halfway through, and use tongs to turn the veggies over for even roasting. Cook until caramelized and tender, 25 to 30 minutes.

Serve.
Transfer the Brussels sprouts and shallots to a serving dish, with lemon wedges to squeeze at the table.

delicious delicata rings

PREP TIME
15 minutes

COOK TIME
30 minutes

SERVES
4

**TOOLS /
EQUIPMENT**
Pointy teaspoon
2 baking sheets
Metal spatula

3 delicata squash, halved widthwise

Olive oil, for drizzling

Flake salt, such as Maldon

Freshly ground black pepper

HELPFUL HINT When choosing delicata squash, look for ones that are firm and heavy for their size.

DID YOU KNOW? Delicata squash have a skin so thin you can eat it, and once roasted, the flesh is so sweet you'd think it was candy. You can store this squash in a cool, dry place away from direct sunlight for up to three months.

Arrange oven racks and preheat oven.
Place one oven rack in the top third of the oven and another in the bottom third, then preheat oven to 425°F.

Prepare the squash.
Use a pointy teaspoon to scrape the seeds and any stringy bits from each squash half and discard (or save for compost). Slice the squash into ½-inch rings, discarding the stem ends.

Prep the squash for roasting.
Drizzle 1 to 2 tablespoons of olive oil onto each baking sheet, and spread it around with your fingers to coat the pans. Lay the delicata rings flat in a single layer on each sheet, and lightly drizzle with olive oil. Season with salt and pepper.

Roast the squash.
Cook for 10 to 15 minutes, until the rings begin to brown on the bottom, then the flip rings to the other side, season again, and swap the pans, returning them to roast for another 10 to 15 minutes, until the squash is tender and deeply golden in spots. Test by seeing if you can pierce them with a fork— if you can, they are ready.

Serve.
Serve warm for a delicious snack or side dish.

Mini Pot Pies (page 161)

6

main dishes

pasta with homemade tomato sauce

PREP TIME
10 minutes

COOK TIME
15 minutes

SERVES
4

TOOLS / EQUIPMENT

Medium saucepan
Paring knife
Slotted spoon
Large bowl
Wooden spoon
Tongs
Large pot
Colander
Fine grater

8 tomatoes—heirloom varieties are ideal, with a few Roma tomatoes in the mix

Ice water

2 tablespoons butter

Olive oil, for drizzling

2 anchovies

2 garlic cloves, sliced thin

Kosher salt

1 pound rigatoni or other ridged pasta

Parmigiano-Reggiano, for serving

Freshly ground black pepper

Blanch tomatoes and peel the skins.

Set a medium saucepan filled with water to boil. Using a paring knife, cut an "X" shape into the bottom of each tomato. Carefully lower 1 or 2 tomatoes into the water at a time and blanch for 1 minute. Use a slotted spoon to transfer the blanched tomatoes to a bowl filled with ice water. When cool enough to handle, peel the skins and discard, then cut larger tomatoes into chunks and smaller ones in half over a bowl to collect their juices. Repeat with the remaining tomatoes, and set aside.

Make the sauce.

In the same saucepan over medium heat, melt the butter and a drizzle of olive oil together. When the butter foams, add the anchovies, letting them sizzle and melt into the buttery mix. Use tongs to break them apart as they dissolve. After a minute or two, add the garlic slices and stir to combine. When the garlic becomes fragrant, add the tomatoes.

Stir the mixture together, and bring to a boil.

Once bubbling, lower the heat to a simmer so the mixture still bubbles, but less vigorously. Stir occasionally, simmering for 7 to 10 minutes, while you cook the pasta.

Cook the pasta.

In a large pot, boil enough water to cook 1 pound of pasta, 2 to 3 quarts. Add 1 tablespoon kosher salt to the water once it reaches a rolling boil, just before adding the pasta. Cook the pasta according to package instructions, stirring immediately after adding it to the water so that the noodles don't stick together. Once the water returns to a boil, stir occasionally until al dente. Drain the pasta in a colander, reserving 1 cupful of the cooking liquid.

Serve.

Add a spoonful or two of the cooking liquid to the sauce and stir to incorporate. Transfer the pasta into shallow bowls, and top with the chunky tomato sauce. Use a fine grater to shower the pasta with a little fresh Parm, followed by salt and pepper to taste. Leftover sauce can be refrigerated for up to 5 days or frozen up to 2 months.

herby pesto pasta

PREP TIME
15 minutes

COOK TIME

10 minutes

SERVES

4

**TOOLS/
EQUIPMENT**

Box grater

Citrus reamer

Food processor

Large pot

Colander

Large bowl

Rubber spatula

Toaster oven

⅓ cup nuts, such as pine nuts, walnuts, almonds, or pistachios

1 garlic clove

½ cup Parmigiano-Reggiano cheese, freshly shredded, plus extra for serving

Olive oil, as needed

2 cups loosely packed fresh basil leaves

½ cup fresh parsley leaves

1 tablespoon kosher salt

1 teaspoon freshly squeezed lemon juice, to prevent oxidizing

1 pound fettuccine

Flake sea salt, such as Maldon

Freshly ground black pepper

Toast the nuts.

Arrange nuts in a single layer on a toaster oven tray. Toast for 4 minutes, or until they become fragrant and their edges turn golden. You may agitate pan halfway through, circulating the them for even toasting. Transfer nuts to a small dish to cool.

Make the pesto.

Using a food processor, pulse the nuts, garlic, cheese, and enough olive oil to make a rough paste. Stop as needed to scrape down the sides of the bowl. Add the basil and parsley, a pinch of salt, and more olive oil, and pulse to combine. The mixture should resemble a bright green sauce. Drizzle the fresh lemon juice over the mixture once you are happy with the consistency.

Boil the pasta.

In a large pot, boil enough water to cook 1 pound of fettuccine, about three quarts (12 cups). Add 1 tablespoon kosher salt to the water once it is at a rolling boil just before adding the pasta. Cook the pasta according to package instructions, stirring immediately after adding the pasta so that it doesn't stick together. Once the water returns to a boil, stir occasionally until al dente. Drain the pasta in a colander, and transfer to a large bowl, reserving 1 cupful of the cooking water for later.

Empty the pesto into the bowl of pasta.

Use a rubber spatula to thoroughly scrape the bowl and underneath the blade, getting all the good bits out. Add a few spoons of the pasta water as you toss the noodles and pesto together. Use a large spoon in one hand and the rubber spatula in the other to combine them well, coating the noodles in the sauce.

Serve.

Twirl tangles of pasta into shallow bowls, spooning additional pesto on top as you like. Shower the pasta with a little more freshly grated cheese, season with salt and pepper, and enjoy at once. Leftover pasta will last up to 3 days, kept sealed in the refrigerator. If you saved any pesto separate from the pasta, transfer it to a jar and cover its surface directly with plastic wrap to slow oxidation, seal it, and keep refrigerated for up to 1 week.

butternut mac 'n' cheese

PREP TIME
20 minutes

COOK TIME
50 minutes

SERVES
4

**TOOLS /
EQUIPMENT**

Box grater

4 ramekins

Toaster oven

Small saucepan

Large pot

Colander

Steamer basket

Tongs

Whisk

Baking sheet

Ladle

Wire cooling rack

4 tablespoons butter, divided, plus more for greasing ramekins

2 thick slices rustic bread, crusts removed and torn into bite-size pieces

½ teaspoon kosher salt, plus a hefty pinch

12 ounces macaroni

½ butternut squash, peeled, seeded, and sliced into inch-long bite-size pieces

2 cups milk

3 tablespoons all-purpose flour

¼ teaspoon freshly grated nutmeg

¼ teaspoon freshly ground black pepper

¼ teaspoon cayenne pepper

1 ½ cups grated sharp white Cheddar cheese, divided

1 cup grated Gruyère cheese, divided

Prepare the ramekins.

Butter 4 ramekins, and set aside on a baking sheet.

Toast the bread.

Place the bread onto a toaster oven tray. In a small saucepan over medium heat, melt 1 tablespoon of butter, and drizzle the butter over the bread, stirring the pieces around the tray to coat. Toast the croutons until lightly crispy, about 5 minutes, and set aside.

Cook the pasta.

Set a large pot filled with water over high heat, and bring to a rolling boil. Add 1 tablespoon salt, add the pasta, and stir well. Cook 3 minutes less than the package instructions say, so that the pasta exterior is cooked and the inside is underdone. Transfer the pasta to a colander, and shake it a few times to drain well. Rinse the pasta briefly to stop it from cooking further and set aside.

Steam the squash.

Fit a steamer basket inside a saucepan and add 1 inch of water. Cover and steam the squash pieces until slightly softened, 3 to 5 minutes. Use tongs to remove the squash from the basket, rinse under cold water, and set aside.

Preheat the oven to 375°F. »

TROUBLESHOOTING
Not keeping your workspace organized when creating a recipe with many steps can backfire on you. This recipe has a number of components to attend to. Pay close attention and they should be a cinch, especially if you keep your workspace uncluttered. Plus, the finished dish is outrageously delicious and well worth the effort!

Make the béchamel.
In a small saucepan over medium-low heat, warm the milk. In the same pot you used for cooking the pasta, over medium heat, melt the remaining 3 tablespoons of butter. When the butter foams, add the flour. Whisk the flour into the butter, stirring to fully combine.

Continue whisking.
Gradually pour in the hot milk. After pouring half in, whisk until the mixture has no lumps, then slowly add the remainder. Whisk constantly, until the mixture bubbles and becomes thick, 8 to 10 minutes.

Combine the ingredients for baking.
Remove the pan from the heat, and stir in the salt, nutmeg, black pepper, cayenne pepper, 1 cup of Cheddar cheese, and ½ cup of Gruyère.

Add pasta and squash.
Stir the cooked pasta and steamed squash into the cheesy béchamel sauce. Ladle the mixture into the ramekins. Sprinkle the remaining ½ cup of Cheddar cheese and ½ cup of Gruyère over the tops, then arrange the toasted croutons on top. Bake until the surfaces are golden, about 25 minutes.

Serve.
Transfer the casseroles to a wire cooling rack, and allow to cool for 5 minutes. Serve the little mac-and-cheese ramekins warm on large plates.

pan-roasted fish

PREP TIME
5 minutes

COOK TIME
10 minutes

SERVES

4

**TOOLS /
EQUIPMENT**

Large cast-iron skillet

Metal spatula

4 (5-ounce) skin-on fish fillets (such as red snapper, flounder, haddock, or salmon), ½ to 1 inch thick

Kosher salt

Freshly ground black pepper

4 tablespoons olive oil

3 tablespoons butter

3 fresh thyme sprigs, leaves stripped from stems, coarsely chopped

Chopped fresh parsley and lemon wedges (optional), for garnish

Prep and season the fillets.

Pat the fish dry with paper towels and season on both sides with salt and pepper.

Sauté the fish.

Place a large cast-iron skillet over high heat. When the skillet is hot, add the oil. Place the fillets skin-side down away from you into the pan, so if any splattering happens, you'll have less risk of being burned. Press down gently with a metal spatula for about 20 seconds around the edges so that the fillets don't curl up.

Lower the heat and continue to cook.

Lower the heat to medium and let sizzle until the fish is caramelized and becoming opaque around the edges, 2 to 3 minutes. Carefully flip the fillets to the second side, and add the butter and thyme to the pan.

Baste the fish.

Tilt the pan slightly to pool the melted butter on one side. Use a spoon to baste the fish with the melted butter. Baste the fillets repeatedly, until they are golden all over and cooked through, 1 minute or so, depending on the thickness of your fish.

Serve.

Serve immediately, with chopped parsley and lemon wedges, if desired.

hearty greens strata

PREP TIME
15 minutes plus
2 hours to soak
and 30 minutes
to sit

COOK TIME
30 minutes

SERVES
4–6

**TOOLS /
EQUIPMENT**

Box grater

Large cast-
iron skillet

Medium bowl

Whisk

Medium glass
or ceramic
baking dish

Baking sheet

Olive oil, for sautéing

1 medium onion, chopped

1 bunch Swiss chard or kale, stems
removed and finely chopped, leaves
coarsely chopped

¼ teaspoon freshly grated nutmeg

Freshly ground black pepper

Kosher salt

5 eggs

1 cup buttermilk

½ cup whole milk

1 tablespoon Dijon mustard

1 ½ cups grated Gruyère cheese

1 cup finely shredded Parmesan cheese

Butter, for greasing

5 slices day-old bread,
cut into large cubes

1 teaspoon red pepper flakes

Sauté vegetables and aromatics.

Into a large cast-iron skillet over medium heat, drizzle enough olive oil to coat the hot pan. Add the onion, and sauté until tender, 5 to 7 minutes. Add the chard stems and nutmeg, and season with black pepper and salt. Stir to incorporate, cooking for another 2 to 3 minutes.

Add the greens and continue cooking.

Add the chard leaves, mix with the other ingredients, and sauté until the leaves have wilted, about 2 minutes. Transfer the mixture to a plate.

Whisk the egg mixture.

In a medium bowl, whisk together the eggs, buttermilk, milk, and mustard.

Combine the cheeses.

In a shallow dish, toss the two cheeses together. Set aside a third of the cheese for final sprinkling before the strata goes into the oven.

Layer the strata.

Butter a medium baking dish well. Arrange a layer of cubed bread. Don't be fussy, a little textural inconsistency will make for pleasing, savory custard layers once the strata is cooked. Add a layer of the onion-greens mixture. Sprinkle a layer of cheese over the surface. Repeat again with each, finishing the top layer with the remaining cubed bread and a sprinkle of red pepper flakes.

delicious additions

Sautéed and added to the mix:

Broccoli

Leeks

Mushrooms

Tomatoes

Zucchini

Saturate the strata.

Carefully pour the egg mixture evenly over the whole surface to saturate the bread layers. Allow the bread to absorb the mixture for at least 2 hours, preferably overnight. If it stands overnight, cover in plastic wrap and refrigerate.

Prepare to bake.

Allow the strata to sit at room temperature for 30 minutes before baking.

Preheat the oven to 350°F.

Bake the strata.

Scatter the reserved cheese on top. Place the strata on a baking sheet and bake uncovered for 30 minutes, or until golden and set in the center.

Serve.

Cool for 10 minutes and serve while still warm. Leftover strata can be kept, refrigerated, for up to 5 days and can be reheated in the toaster oven.

tomato soup with broiled cheesy toasts

PREP TIME
10 minutes

COOK TIME
35 minutes

TOTAL TIME
1 hour

SERVES
4

TOOLS / EQUIPMENT

Box grater

Paring knife

Medium saucepan

Slotted spoon

Large bowl

Dutch oven

Immersion blender

Wooden spoon

Toaster oven

Ladle

4 cups tomatoes (6 to 8 medium tomatoes), skins peeled, chopped

1 tablespoon olive oil, plus more for drizzling

2 tablespoons butter

1 medium onion, chopped

½ teaspoon freshly grated nutmeg

½ teaspoon smoked paprika

Sea salt

Freshly ground black pepper

2 cups chicken stock

FOR THE TOASTS

4 slices country loaf

½ cup grated Gruyère cheese

Blanch the tomatoes and peel the skins.

Set a medium saucepan filled with water to boil. With your knife, cut an "X" into the bottoms of the tomatoes. Carefully lower 2 tomatoes into the water at a time and blanch for 1 minute. Use a slotted spoon to transfer the blanched tomatoes to a large bowl filled with ice water. When cool enough to handle, peel the skins and discard, then slice the tomatoes into large chunks over a bowl to collect their juices. Repeat with the remaining tomatoes, and add them to the bowl.

Make the soup.

In a Dutch oven or other heavy-bottomed pot over medium heat, heat the oil and butter, and swirl the pan to coat. Sauté the onion until translucent, 5 to 7 minutes. Add the tomatoes and their juice, and bring to a boil. Lower the heat, and simmer, stirring occasionally, for about 5 minutes.

Incorporate the spices and stock, and continue cooking.

Add the nutmeg and paprika, season with salt and pepper, and add the stock. Stir to incorporate, return the heat to medium, and bring to bubbling again. Lower the heat and simmer with the lid on for 20 to 25 minutes. ➤➤

TRY INSTEAD For a creamier soup, add ⅔ cup heavy cream and then purée it. Or, swap a dollop of crème fraîche for the toast.

FOOD FACT This soup stores well and tastes even better the second day. You can keep it in the refrigerator for up to five days, as long as you bring it to a boil every two days. You can freeze it as well, and there it keeps for up to three months.

Purée the soup.
Remove the pot from heat, take the lid off, and let cool for at least 15 minutes. Pulse an immersion blender to purée the soup. Always keep the blender fully submerged in the liquid while puréeing to avoid an enormous mess, and most important, to avoid being burned. Blend thoroughly for a creamy consistency, less if you prefer it chunky.

Make the broiled toasts.
Toast the bread in a toaster oven until crisp, about 5 minutes. Divide the grated cheese evenly between the slices, turn the toaster oven to broil, return the toasts, and broil until the cheese is melted and bubbling, about 3 minutes more.

Serve.
Ladle the soup into bowls, and top with the cheesy toasts. Drizzle with olive oil, add pepper, and eat at once.

chicken skewer sandwiches

PREP TIME
20 minutes, plus
overnight to
marinate

COOK TIME
20 minutes

SERVES
4

**TOOLS /
EQUIPMENT**

Citrus reamer

Zester

Bread knife

Large bowl

Metal skewers

Tongs

Grill pan

⅔ cup olive oil, plus extra for drizzling

⅓ cup red wine vinegar

2 lemons, juiced, and one zested

4 garlic cloves, chopped

1 tablespoon fresh thyme leaves

1 tablespoon fresh oregano leaves

1 tablespoon fresh basil leaves, rolled
and chiffonaded (see Summery Corn
and Watermelon Salad, page 112)

1 teaspoon red pepper flakes, or
to taste

1 bay leaf

1 teaspoon cane sugar

1 teaspoon kosher salt

1 teaspoon freshly ground
black pepper

1 pound boneless chicken thighs,
cut into 1½-inch cubes

1 baguette, cut into 4 sections, each
split open lengthwise

1 tablespoon coarsely chopped fresh
mint or parsley, or a mix, for garnish

Make the marinade.

In a large bowl, stir together the olive oil, vinegar,
lemon juice and zest, garlic, thyme, oregano, basil,
red pepper flakes, bay leaf, sugar, salt, and pepper.
Add the cubed chicken and refrigerate, covered
tightly or in a large, resealable bag, overnight to
marinate.

Grill the skewers.

Thread the chicken onto skewers, folding the
meat on itself to skewer if it is uneven. Heat a grill
pan over high heat until hot. Grill the chicken for
3 to 5 minutes per side, until cooked through and
charred in spots.

Grill the bread.

Transfer the grilled skewers to a large plate while
you grill the bread. Drizzle olive oil onto the bread
and grill for 3 to 5 minutes apiece, rotating as
needed, until blackened in spots.

Serve.

These skewers are delicious laid on top of the
grilled bread with a scatter of chopped fresh
herbs—like parsley or mint—to garnish.

 HELPFUL HINT Plan ahead: This recipe
requires marinating overnight. This
marinade also is great with pork, beef, and
lamb as well as chicken.

winter white bean stew

PREP TIME
20 minutes
plus 6 hours
to soak

COOK TIME
1 hour

SERVES
4–6

**TOOLS /
EQUIPMENT**

Large bowl

Dutch oven

Aluminum foil

Small baking dish

Food processor

Wooden spoon

Ladle

Rubber spatula

3 cups dry white beans, such as cannellini, flageolet, or northern beans, or a mix

2 bay leaves

2 Parmigiano-Reggiano rinds or 2 small Parmesan wedges

1 head garlic

2 tablespoons olive oil, plus more for drizzling

1 jalapeño

Kosher salt

Freshly ground black pepper

2 small onions, chopped

5 to 7 small carrots, chopped

3 celery stalks, chopped

1 tablespoon finely chopped fresh rosemary quills

1 teaspoon red pepper flakes

1 cup chicken stock or water

Crusty bread, for serving

Prepare the beans.

In a large enough bowl for them to double in volume (more than one, if using different beans), soak the dry beans in enough cold water to cover by at least 2 inches. After soaking for 6 hours or overnight, drain and rinse, then transfer to a Dutch oven or other large, heavy-bottomed stewpot. Rinse the bowl, and set it aside.

Preheat the oven to 375°F.

Cook the beans.

Place the stewpot over high heat and add enough water to cover the beans by at least 2 inches. Add the bay leaves and cheese rinds, and bring the water to a boil. Once the water is bubbling, lower the heat, and cook the beans on a low simmer for 45 minutes to an hour, until the beans are tender.

Roast the garlic and jalapeño.

While the beans cook, cut the top third off the head of garlic. Nestle it in a sheet of aluminum foil, and drizzle olive oil over it. Fold the foil to seal the garlic, and place in a small baking dish. Do the same with the jalapeño in a small baking dish. Roast the two in the oven for as long as you cook the beans, then remove and set aside to cool.

Transfer the beans and sauté the veggies.

When the beans are finished cooking, they will still look a little soupy. Pull out the cheese rinds and discard, and carefully transfer the beans back into the soaking bowl. Season with salt and pepper, and set aside.

Cook the aromatics.

Return the pot to the burner on medium heat. Add the olive oil and onions, and sauté, stirring occasionally. As they start to become translucent, add the carrots and celery, as well as the rosemary and red pepper flakes. Sauté, stirring occasionally, for 7 minutes. Season with salt and pepper.

Purée the beans with the stock and the aromatics.

In a food processor, pulse together 2 cups of the cooked bean mixture, the roasted jalapeño minus its stem, the chicken stock, and the cloves squeezed out of half the head of roasted garlic until creamy. (You will have a half-head of roasted garlic leftover, which can be used in other soups or whipped into yogurt or cream cheese and spread on toast.) This mixture will add body to the finished stew.

Stir to combine.

Empty the purée into the veggie pot, along with the bowl of cooked beans and their liquid, and give it all a good stir.

Serve.

If the stew needs to be rewarmed, do so over medium-low heat, then ladle the stew into wide bowls and enjoy with crusty bread. Any leftovers can be refrigerated for up to 1 week, or frozen for up to 2 months.

fresh fish tacos

PREP TIME
15 minutes
plus 50 minutes
to marinate

COOK TIME
15 minutes

SERVES
4

**TOOLS /
EQUIPMENT**

Small sauté pan

Small mason jar
with lid

Mortar and pestle

Small bowl

Baking sheet

Aluminum foil

Tea towel

FOR QUICK-PICKLED ONIONS

½ red onion, sliced thin

Pinch black peppercorns

1 bay leaf

¾ cup white vinegar

[INGREDIENT LIST CONTINUES ON NEXT PAGE]

Marinate the onion.

In a small mason jar with a lid, arrange the onion slices, adding a pinch of peppercorns and a bay leaf, and pour in enough white vinegar to cover. Set aside to marinate for at least 30 minutes.

Marinate the fish.

Grind the toasted cumin into a coarse powder with a mortar and pestle. In a small bowl, mix the olive oil, chili powder, cumin, chopped cilantro, and jalapeño, and season with salt. Place the fillets on a baking sheet and pour the marinade over, making sure to coat the fillets well on both sides. Marinate for 20 minutes at room temperature.

Cook the fish.

Heat the broiler with the oven rack in the highest position. Season the fish with salt and pepper. Broil until the fillets are browned on top and the flesh is opaque throughout, about 5 minutes. Remove the pan from the oven and flake the fish with a fork. Taste and adjust seasoning as needed, then set aside.

Heat the tortillas.

Lower the oven temperature to 400°F. Place the tortillas in two stacks of 4, and wrap the bundles in aluminum foil. Heat in the oven for 7 to 10 minutes, until the tortillas are warmed through. Place the tortillas, still wrapped in foil, in a tea towel to keep warm. »

fresh fish tacos, continued

FOR THE TACOS

1 teaspoon cumin seeds, toasted (see the No-Nonsense Guacamole, page 101)

⅓ cup olive oil

1½ teaspoons chili powder

¼ cup chopped fresh cilantro leaves, plus more for garnish

½ to 1 jalapeño pepper, seeded and minced

Kosher salt

1 pound flaky white fish (such as flounder, red snapper, or cod), cut into 4 pieces

Freshly ground black pepper

8 fresh corn or flour tortillas

1 recipe of Salsa Fresca (page 46) and/or Savory Cabbage Slaw (page 110), for serving

Sour cream, for serving

2 limes, quartered

Assemble and serve:

To assemble the tacos, place a heaping spoonful of Savory Cabbage Slaw on the center of a tortilla. Add the flaked fish and Salsa Fresca, and top with the marinated onions. Serve accompanied by cilantro sprigs, sour cream, and lime wedges.

 PRO TIP You will most likely have leftover pickled onions. Keep them submerged in the vinegar in a refrigerated airtight container. You can then use the vinegar for other cooking, such as in salad dressings, and the pickled onions on anything from scrambled eggs to grilled chicken. Both will keep for several weeks.

miso-grilled shrimp skewers

PREP TIME
20 minutes plus
20 minutes to
marinate

COOK TIME
5–7 minutes

SERVES
4

**TOOLS /
EQUIPMENT**

Citrus reamer

Fine grater

Large bowl

Whisk

Grill pan

Metal skewers

2 tablespoons freshly squeezed lime juice, with extra wedges for garnish

2 tablespoons mirin

2 tablespoons yellow miso

1 tablespoon sesame oil

1 tablespoon fresh ginger, peeled and finely grated

1 large garlic clove, finely grated

1 pound large shrimp, shelled and deveined

**OPTIONAL EXTRAS,
FOR SERVING**

Chopped scallions

Sunflower sprouts

Green beans, steamed and crunchy

Sliced English or Persian cucumbers

Salad greens

Fresh cilantro leaves

Cooked rice or steamed buns

Make the glaze.

In a large bowl, whisk together the lime juice, mirin, miso, sesame oil, ginger, and garlic. Add the shrimp, and toss to coat. Let marinate for 20 minutes.

Grill the shrimp.

Preheat a grill pan over medium-high heat. Thread the shrimp onto metal skewers, piercing the shrimp at the tail end and at the thickest part of the body to secure. Grill the shrimp over medium-high heat until lightly charred and opaque, turning once, about 5 minutes.

Serve.

These glazed and grilled shrimp are great served in steamed buns with chopped fresh scallions and cilantro, over rice, or alongside crunchy green beans, greens, or Asian Cucumber Salad (page 111).

> DID YOU KNOW? Miso and mirin are staples in Japanese cuisine. Miso paste is made from fermented soybeans, sometimes with the addition of rice, barley, or wheat, and is rich in vitamin B and protein. Mirin is a sweet, golden Japanese wine made from rice. Both are available at Asian markets or the Asian food section at specialty grocers as well as online.

spring rolls and dipping sauces

PREP TIME
35 minutes

COOK TIME
5 minutes

SERVES
4

TOOLS / EQUIPMENT

Citrus reamer

Box grater

2 small bowls

Small saucepan

Whisk

Medium saucepan

Colander

Large bowl

Dish towel

FOR THE DIPPING SAUCES

4 teaspoons fish sauce

¼ cup water

2 tablespoons freshly squeezed lime juice

1 small garlic clove, grated

1 teaspoon cane sugar

½ teaspoon chili sauce (such as sambal oelek); less if you prefer less spice

2 tablespoons crunchy peanut butter

4 tablespoons hoisin sauce

[INGREDIENT LIST CONTINUES ON NEXT PAGE]

Make the two sauces.

In a small bowl, stir together the ingredients for the first sauce: fish sauce, water, lime juice, garlic, sugar, and chili sauce. Set aside. In a small saucepan over medium heat, mix together ingredients for the second sauce: peanut butter and hoisin sauce. Add a few spoonfuls of water to thin the sauce slightly, and whisk until incorporated. Transfer to another small bowl, and set aside.

Prep the vermicelli.

In a medium saucepan, soak the rice noodles in hot water until they turn opaque and soften. You may turn on the heat to expedite this, but do not boil them, as they may become soggy. Transfer the noodles to a colander and rinse under cold water. Drain and set aside.

Prep the wrappers.

Have enough "bathwater-warm" water in a bowl large enough so that when you dip the wrappers, the water comes up halfway. Dunk and lift, rotate a quarter-turn, and repeat until you have gone all the way around with the wrapper. The time spent dunking takes maybe 2 seconds total, as you are only trying to soften it. With this method, the wrapper becomes pliable but isn't as likely to tear.

FOR THE ROLLS

1 ounce rice vermicelli

Hot water, for soaking

8 rice wrappers (8½-inch diameter)

12 large shrimp, peeled, cooked, and halved lengthwise

2 tablespoons fresh Thai basil leaves

3 tablespoons fresh mint leaves

3 tablespoons fresh cilantro leaves

2 lettuce leaves (such as butter or romaine), halved

½ cup mung bean sprouts

1 carrot, julienned

FOOD FACT Vermicelli often comes in 2-ounce bundles, but using it all makes for a noodle-heavy spring roll. Cook the bundle, and save the remainder for another use.

TRY INSTEAD Swap the shrimp for sautéed chicken breast, thinly sliced into 8 pieces. Swap the mung beans for half a hothouse cucumber, cut into thin strips. Swap the Thai basil for regular basil. And add more crunch with julienned celery, radishes, cabbage, or jicama.

Assemble the rolls.

Place the wet wrapper on a damp dish towel laid flat on your work surface. Arrange 3 shrimp halves pink-side down followed by a pinch of the Thai basil, mint, and cilantro leaves, then a cluster of the crunchy elements: lettuce, bean sprouts, and carrots, then a small handful of vermicelli, folding the length of noodles back and forth until you have a neat pile. Leave a 2-inch border on either side as you layer the ingredients.

Bundle the ingredients, and roll.

Your aim is to make a tight bundle when rolling. Gently pull the edge of the wrapper up over the fillings. Simultaneously use your fingers to press the fillings into a small bundle under the wrapper. Compressing them into a little bundle will keep all the ingredients together and help the roll remain firm and even.

Create a firm seal.

Roll away from you, and tuck the fillings toward you. After a full rotation, fold the sides of the wrapper in. Continue rolling to the edge, gathering fillings in until the roll is sealed.

Serve.

Spring rolls can be served whole with dipping sauces on the side or cut on the diagonal to display their colorful fillings. Refrigerate the finished rolls for up to 2 hours before serving, each wrapped individually in plastic wrap. The rice wrappers will toughen if stored longer than a few hours, increasing their likelihood of cracking.

sopa de lima (chicken lime soup)

PREP TIME
20 minutes

COOK TIME
30 minutes

SERVES
4–6

TOOLS / EQUIPMENT

Fine grater

Citrus reamer

Large cast-iron skillet

Wooden spoon

Tongs

Slotted spoon

Wire cooling rack

Large bowl

Ladle

Safflower oil, for frying

3 corn tortillas, cut into ¼-inch strips

Flake salt, such as Maldon

1 white onion, chopped

4 bone-in, skinless chicken thighs

3 Roma tomatoes, cored

1 serrano or jalapeño chili, cored, seeded, and chopped

½ teaspoon dried thyme

2 garlic cloves, finely grated

3 cups chicken stock

Juice of 3 limes, plus 2 cut into wedges for serving

1½ cups frozen peas, blanched

2 avocados, sliced or cubed, for garnish

Fresh cilantro leaves, for garnish

Freshly ground black pepper

Fry the tortilla strips.
Into a large cast-iron skillet, pour enough oil so that it comes up a quarter inch. Heat the oil, and when very hot, fry the tortilla strips in small batches until golden and crisp, 30 seconds to 1 minute per batch. Tortilla strips should sizzle immediately upon contact with the oil, but not burn. If the oil is smoking, lower the heat.

Transfer the tortilla strips.
Use a slotted spoon or tongs to transfer the fried tortillas to a paper towel-lined wire cooling rack to soak up excess oil. Sprinkle with a pinch of salt. Repeat until all the tortilla strips have been fried. Set the tortilla strips aside and reserve the oil.

Sauté the onion and the chicken.
In a large saucepan over medium heat, use 1 tablespoon of the frying oil to sauté the onion until translucent, about 5 minutes. Add another tablespoon of the oil, and brown the chicken thighs, turning to brown all sides.

Simmer the soup.
Add the tomatoes, jalapeño, thyme, garlic, and stock, and bring the mixture to a boil. Reduce the heat to simmer and cook for 20 minutes, or until the chicken is cooked through, breaking up the tomatoes with the edge of a wooden spoon halfway through simmering.

Shred the meat.

Remove the saucepan from the heat. Use tongs to transfer the chicken from the soup into a large bowl. When cool enough to handle, discard the bones and shred the meat, either with your fingers or using two forks. Return the shredded chicken to the soup, and add the lime juice and peas. Stir thoroughly to combine, taste, and adjust the seasoning as needed.

Serve.

Ladle the soup into bowls, and top with the avocado, cilantro leaves, and fried tortillas. Squeeze the lime wedges over the soup and eat immediately. Allow any leftover soup to come to room temperature, and store refrigerated in sealed containers for up to 3 days. Fried tortilla strips will keep at room temperature, stored between layers of parchment and sealed, for 2 days. Reheat tortillas in the toaster oven or a sauté pan.

roasted chicken with onions and lemons

PREP TIME
10 minutes

COOK TIME
55 minutes

TOTAL TIME
1 hour,
20 minutes

SERVES

4

**TOOLS/
EQUIPMENT**

Large cast-
iron skillet

Tongs

Slotted spoon

Large plate

1 (3- to 4-pound) whole chicken

Sea salt

Freshly ground black pepper

1 tablespoon olive oil, plus more
for drizzling

4 onions, cut into wedges

5 lemons, halved

1 head garlic, top third cut off

5 fresh thyme sprigs

Preheat the oven to 425°F.

Season the chicken.
Season the entire chicken well with salt and pepper.
Turn it over to season the backside as well as under-
neath the wings and inside the cavity.

Brown the chicken.
Heat a large cast-iron skillet over medium-high heat,
add the olive oil, and cook the chicken, breast-side
down, until golden brown. Use tongs and a slotted
spoon to gently turn the chicken, being careful not
to tear the skin. Brown on all sides, 10 to 15 minutes
total, and transfer to a plate.

Prep the chicken for roasting.
In the same skillet, layer the onions in the center, so
they'll be underneath the chicken as you roast it.
They will soak up the fat and juices, which will make
them tender and super flavorful. Add the lemon
halves, cut-side down, and the garlic and thyme.
Drizzle everything with olive oil.

Roast the chicken.
Place the chicken back in the skillet, atop the onion
pile. Roast until a meat thermometer inserted into
the thickest part of the thigh registers 165°F, 35 to
40 minutes. Another way to see if the chicken is
ready is to cut into the thigh meat at the joint. If the
juices run clear, it's ready.

TROUBLESHOOTING

Taking the bird directly from the refrigerator to the flame will increase its roasting time and cause it to cook unevenly. Before cooking a chicken (or any meat), let it come to room temperature, about 30 minutes or so. Another frequent mistake is not properly drying the chicken before roasting it. There's no need to rinse the chicken if it's fresh—and doing so only increases your chances of getting a soggy skin. Instead, remove the chicken from any packaging and thoroughly pat it dry.

Serve.

Before cutting into the chicken, let it rest for 10 to 15 minutes, allowing the internal juices to reabsorb. The roasted chicken is great served alongside the tender caramelized veggies. Spoon the pan juices over all and enjoy!

HELPFUL HINT
Not only does a generous sprinkling of salt make chicken taste good, it helps make for a crispy golden-brown skin.

mini pot pies

PREP TIME
15 minutes

COOK TIME
1 hour

TOTAL TIME
1 hour,
25 minutes

SERVES
4

**TOOLS /
EQUIPMENT**

Vegetable peeler

Rolling pin

Parchment paper

Baking sheet

Large cast-
iron skillet

Whisk

Ladle

4 ramekins

Pastry brush

1 sheet frozen puff pastry, such as Dufour brand, thawed in refrigerator

2 tablespoons all-purpose flour, plus more for dusting surface

4 tablespoons unsalted butter

1 shallot, finely chopped

2 teaspoons fresh thyme leaves

1 cup low-sodium chicken broth

1 cup whole milk

Kosher salt

Freshly ground black pepper

4 carrots, peeled and sliced

3 cups shredded or diced leftover chicken or turkey

1 cup frozen peas, thawed

1 cup white pearl onions, peeled

¼ cup chopped fresh flat-leaf parsley

Hot sauce, to taste

1 egg, lightly beaten

Preheat the oven to 400°F.

Roll out the pastry.
Unfold the pastry, and gently roll it out on a lightly floured work surface to ¼ inch thick. Cut it into 4 equal-size pieces slightly larger than the size of your ramekins. Lay them out onto parchment paper, transfer to a baking sheet, and refrigerate until ready to use.

Make the roux.
In a large cast-iron skillet over medium heat, heat the butter. When it is melted and bubbling, add the shallot and thyme, and cook until the shallot becomes translucent, about 4 minutes, stirring regularly. Add the flour and cook, whisking constantly, until the mixture is golden and fully incorporated, about 5 minutes.

Add the remaining ingredients.
Whisk in the broth gradually, incorporating the first half completely before adding the remainder. Whisk in the milk, and season with salt and pepper. Bring to a boil, then reduce heat and simmer, whisking occasionally, until the mixture is thick enough to coat a spoon, 10 to 12 minutes. Add the carrots and cook until just tender, 3 to 5 minutes. Add the chicken, peas, onions, and parsley. Season with hot sauce, salt, and pepper, and stir to combine.

Prepare the ramekins.

Ladle the mixture into 4 ramekins or mini casseroles assembled on a baking sheet. Drape puff pastry over filling, ensuring that it hangs over ramekin edges. Gently press on the edges to seal. Brush the pastry with the beaten egg, and make a slit in the centers with a sharp knife for steam to escape while baking.

Bake the pot pies.

Bake until the puff pastry surfaces are golden and the filling is bubbling through the slits, 15 to 20 minutes. Reduce the heat to 350°F, and bake until the puff pastry is deeply golden and cooked through, 10 to 15 minutes longer.

Serve.

Let sit for 10 minutes before serving on large plates.

PRO TIP For an extra-special effect, use a small cookie cutter in place of cutting a simple steam vent. Press the cookie cutter into the center of the cold pastry sections. When assembling the pot pies, wet the back of the pastry cookie cutter shape with a little water and press into the pastry, next to its cutout.

turkey pan bagnat

PREP TIME
15 minutes
plus 20 minutes
to weight down

COOK TIME
none

SERVES
4

TOOLS/ EQUIPMENT

Small bowl

Bread knife

Whisk

Plastic wrap

Cast-iron skillet

FOR THE DRESSING

2 tablespoons Dijon mustard

1 tablespoon mayonnaise

1 teaspoon red wine vinegar

¼ cup chopped fresh parsley

1 tablespoon olive oil

FOR THE SANDWICH

1 (10-inch) loaf ciabatta bread

1 handful haricots verts, blanched, cut into bite-size pieces

1 cup roasted red pepper strips

½ small red onion, sliced thin

Flake salt, such as Maldon

Freshly ground black pepper

8 ounces thinly sliced roasted turkey breast

½ cup pesto (page 136)

Make the dressing.

In a small bowl, whisk together the mustard, mayonnaise, vinegar, parsley, and olive oil. Set aside.

Assemble the sandwich.

Slice the ciabatta in half horizontally. Partially hollow out the bottom half and set it on plastic wrap large enough to wrap the sandwich. Place a layer of each of the following on the bread in this order: dressing, haricots verts, roasted pepper, and sliced onion. Season with salt and pepper. Drizzle the dressing all over, then add the turkey.

Weight down the sandwich.

Spread the top half with pesto, place it on to the sandwich, and wrap tightly in plastic. Put the wrapped sandwich in a resealable plastic bag, squeezing out any air before sealing. Place a cast-iron skillet on the sandwich to press for 10 minutes. Turn the sandwich over and press it again for another 10 minutes.

Serve.

Before serving, remove the weight, unwrap the sandwich, and let it come to room temperature, or keep it wrapped and weighted in the refrigerator for 8 hours or overnight. This extra time weighted allows the flavors to meld. Cut into four sections.

> TRY INSTEAD Swap the roasted peppers for hard-cooked eggs, the turkey for quality canned tuna, and the pesto for artichokes. Voila! You have the traditional pan bagnat, which literally means "bathed bread."

pulled pork sliders

PREP TIME
15 minutes plus
1 hour to rest

COOK TIME
3 hours,
40 minutes

TOTAL TIME
5 hours,
15 minutes

SERVES
8

**TOOLS /
EQUIPMENT**

Small cast-
iron skillet

Mortar and pestle

Small bowl

Plastic wrap

Tray

Aluminum foil

Baking sheet

Large bowl

Tongs

2 teaspoons whole coriander seeds

2 teaspoons whole cumin seeds

2 tablespoons dark brown sugar

1 tablespoon kosher salt

1 teaspoon freshly ground
black pepper

1 tablespoon paprika

1½ teaspoons dry mustard powder

¼ teaspoon ground cayenne pepper

1 (6- to 8-pound) bone-in pork shoulder,
preferably skin-on

½ cup apple cider vinegar

2 tablespoons cane sugar

Pinch red pepper flakes

Toasted buns, for serving

1 recipe Savory Cabbage Slaw
(page 110), for serving

Toast the spices.

In a small, dry cast-iron skillet over medium heat, toast the coriander and cumin until fragrant, about 1 to 2 minutes. Use a mortar and pestle to grind the toasted spices into a powder.

Assemble the spice rub.

In a small bowl, mix together the brown sugar, salt, pepper, coriander, cumin, paprika, mustard powder, and cayenne in a small bowl, mixing with your fingers or a fork until well combined.

Season the meat and let it rest.

Rub the spice mixture over the entire surface of the pork, caking as much of it onto the meat as you can. If you have time, let the meat rest 1 to 2 hours at room temperature before roasting, or refrigerate overnight, loosely wrapped in plastic and set on a tray.

Preheat the oven to 325°F.

But first, adjust the oven rack to the lower-middle position.

Roast the pork.

Place the pork on a foil-lined, rimmed baking sheet, skin-side-up, and roast for 3 to 3½ hours, or until the meat is pull-apart tender.

Let it rest.

Transfer the pork to a large bowl, and let it rest at least 20 minutes. »

pulled pork sliders, continued

Roast the pork skin.

Use tongs to carefully lift the skin off. Raise the oven temperature to 500°F. Use a fork to scrape any clinging meat into the bowl. Remove the fat from the skin and discard, returning the skin to the baking sheet. Roast the skin for 5 to 10 minutes, until crisp and bubbly. Remove from the oven and set aside.

Shred the meat.

Shred the pork using two forks or your hands. Save bones for stock or discard. Finely chop the skin, and combine it with the meat, removing any visible fat. Season the meat with salt and pepper. Stir together the vinegar, cane sugar, and a pinch of red pepper flakes, and add to the mixture to taste.

Serve.

Serve the pulled pork hot, piled on toasted buns and topped with Savory Cabbage Slaw. Store the pulled pork for up to 4 days refrigerated in a sealed container. It also keeps frozen for up to 1 month.

DID YOU KNOW? This cut is often called "pork butt," even though it's actually the shoulder. The word *butt* comes from Old English and means "the widest part." On a pig, the widest part is the shoulder, not its actual hindquarters. And that's why it's called the butt!

minty lamb burgers

PREP TIME
10 minutes

COOK TIME
12–15 minutes

SERVES
4

**TOOLS /
EQUIPMENT**
Fine grater
Medium bowl
Pastry brush
Grill pan
Tongs
Bread knife

1½ pounds ground lamb

1 garlic clove, finely grated

3 tablespoons finely chopped fresh mint

3 tablespoons finely chopped fresh parsley

½ teaspoon cumin seeds, toasted and ground in a mortar and pestle (see No-Nonsense Guacamole, page 101)

Kosher salt

Freshly ground black pepper

Olive oil, for brushing

Ciabatta rolls, for serving

Easy Tzatziki (page 95), for serving

Romaine lettuce leaves, for serving

delicious additions

Feta cheese, sliced thin

Red onion, sliced thin

Make the patties.

In a medium bowl, gently mix together the lamb with the garlic, mint, parsley, cumin, and a pinch each of salt and pepper. Divide the meat into 4 patties of equal size and thickness—about ½ inch thick—and transfer to a plate. Press a small dimple in the center of each patty with two fingers to offset how it shrinks as it cooks. Lightly brush the burgers with olive oil, and season again with salt and pepper.

Cook the burgers.

Heat the grill pan over high heat. When it's hot, brush the grate lightly with olive oil. Grill the patties over medium heat for 7 to 8 minutes for medium-rare or 8 to 10 minutes for medium, turning halfway through. Transfer them to a plate.

Grill the bread.

Slice the ciabatta in half horizontally, brush lightly with olive oil, and place cut-side down on the grill pan. Grill long enough to allow the bread to char in spots, 3 to 5 minutes.

Serve.

Put the bread on plates and top with the burgers. Garnish with the Easy Tzatziki, romaine, and any delicious additions.

> HELPFUL HINT Handle the ground lamb lightly and don't pack the patty too densely, or else the burger will be tough, not tender.

savory beef ragù

PREP TIME
15 minutes

COOK TIME
1 hour
40 minutes

SERVES
4

**TOOLS /
EQUIPMENT**
Fine grater
Dutch oven
Wooden spoon

2 strips thick-cut bacon, diced

1 onion, chopped

2 carrots, scrubbed and chopped

2 celery stalks, chopped

4 garlic cloves, finely grated

1 fennel bulb, sliced

3 anchovy filets

1 pound ground beef

½ cup dry red wine

2 fresh thyme sprigs, leaves stripped
from stems

1 bay leaf

½ teaspoon red chili flakes

⅛ teaspoon freshly grated nutmeg

⅛ teaspoon ground cinnamon

1 (28-ounce) can whole plum tomatoes

1 tablespoon tomato paste

1 cup beef stock

2 teaspoons balsamic vinegar

2 teaspoons Worcestershire sauce

Kosher salt

Freshly ground black pepper

Cook the bacon.

In a Dutch oven or other heavy-bottomed pot over medium heat, cook the bacon until just crispy, about 7 minutes. Remove the bacon from the fat, and set aside.

Cook the vegetables.

Sauté the onion in the bacon fat until translucent, stirring occasionally, about 10 minutes. Add the carrots and celery, stir to combine, and cook for another 5 minutes or until lightly browned. Add the garlic, fennel, and anchovies, making a little room at the base of the pot for the anchovies. As they begin to sizzle, break the anchovies up with the edge of a wooden spoon and stir to incorporate.

Add the remaining ingredients.

Add the ground beef and bacon to the pot. Sauté until lightly browned, 5 to 7 minutes, stirring and breaking up meat as you did the anchovies. Add the wine, and as it bubbles, scrape the bottom of the pot to free up any browned bits. Reduce the wine by half, stirring occasionally, then add the thyme, bay leaf, chili flakes, nutmeg, cinnamon, tomatoes, tomato paste, beef stock, vinegar, and Worcestershire sauce. Give a good stir to bring the mixture together.

Bring the ragù to a simmer.
Taste, season with salt and pepper as needed, and cover. Turn the heat to low so that it bubbles slowly. After 10 minutes or so, break the softened tomatoes into chunks using the edge of a wooden spoon.

Continue to simmer.
Cover again and simmer for another 45 minutes to 1 hour, or until the ingredients have melded and the sauce has thickened. Season with salt and pepper.

Serve.
Serve hot directly from the pot set on a trivet at the table. This dish is fantastic tossed with cooked pasta or alongside crusty bread.

Coconut Ice Pops (page 179)

7

desserts

dreamy cheesecake

PREP TIME
20 minutes plus
3 hours to chill

COOK TIME
1 hour

SERVES
10

**TOOLS/
EQUIPMENT**

Zester
Resealable bag
Rolling pin
Medium bowl
Rubber spatula
Springform pan
Electric mixer
Large bowl
Small bowl
Baking sheet

FOR THE CRUST

1 packet whole wheat graham
crackers (9 crackers)

1 teaspoon ground cinnamon

3 tablespoons cane sugar

½ teaspoon kosher salt

⅓ cup butter, melted

FOR THE CAKE

2 (8-ounce) packages cream cheese,
at room temperature

¼ teaspoon pure vanilla extract

1 teaspoon finely grated lemon zest

1¼ cups cane sugar

2 tablespoons all-purpose flour

¼ teaspoon kosher salt

5 whole eggs, plus 1 egg yolk

¼ cup heavy cream

Make the crust.

Put the graham crackers in a resealable plastic bag. With a rolling pin, crush the crackers into crumbs. If you prefer a finer crust, continue crushing the crackers until you've reached a texture you like. In a medium bowl, mix together the crushed graham crackers, cinnamon, sugar, and salt. Pour in the melted butter, and stir to combine.

Form and set the crust.

Use a rubber spatula or the back of a spoon to spread and compress the mixture evenly into a 9-inch springform pan. Press the crust a little up the sides of the pan, ensuring the crust is even at its base and thins as it goes up. Chill in the refrigerator to set while you make the filling.

Preheat the oven to 500°F.

Mix the filling.

In a large bowl, beat the cheese with an electric mixer until fluffy. Add the vanilla and lemon zest, and mix to combine.

Combine the remaining ingredients.

In a small bowl, stir together the sugar, flour, and salt. Gradually blend the dry ingredients into the cheese. One at a time, add the eggs and additional yolk, whipping to combine and pausing after each to scrape down the sides of the bowl. Gently incorporate the cream, and whip to combine.

Bake the cake.

Pour the mixture into the crust. Place on a baking sheet, and bake for 5 to 8 minutes. Lower the temperature to 200°F, and bake for about 45 to 55 minutes more, until the edges are golden and the center still jiggles. Turn the oven off, and with the door ajar, allow the cheesecake to cool inside for about an hour. Refrigerate for 3 hours, up to overnight.

Serve.

Remove the cake from the refrigerator. Run a butter knife around the inside edge to loosen the cake from the pan. Open the springform pan, remove the cake, and serve at once.

flognarde (apple-custard bake)

PREP TIME
15 minutes

COOK TIME
30 minutes

SERVES
4

TOOLS / EQUIPMENT

Zester

Vegetable peeler

Large cast-iron skillet

Medium bowl

Whisk

4 tablespoons butter, cubed, plus more for greasing the pan

5 tablespoons flour

4 tablespoons sugar

Zest of 2 Meyer lemons

⅔ cup whole milk

4 eggs

3 apples, peeled, cored, and cut into ½-inch wedges

Confectioners' sugar, for dusting

Grease the pan.
Butter a cast-iron skillet.

Preheat the oven to 400°F.

Mix the ingredients:
In a medium bowl, mix together the flour, sugar, lemon zest, and milk. Add the eggs and beat vigorously. Continue whisking as you pour the mixture into the pan.

Arrange the fruit.
Fan the apple wedges and lay them onto the mixture. It's okay if they slide a little as you arrange them.

Bake the custard.
Dot the surface with butter, and bake until the custard puffs and has turned golden brown at the edges, about 30 minutes.

Serve.
Dust confectioners' sugar onto the custard. Serve hot or at room temperature, cut into wedges.

> **TRY INSTEAD** Substitute sliced pears or peaches for the apples. Or include a scatter of raisins, grapes, or cherries in the mix.

> **DID YOU KNOW?** *Flognarde* originated in the Auvergne region of France. This dessert goes by different names based on the region it's made in and the toppings added.

peach-blueberry crisp

PREP TIME
10 minutes

COOK TIME
45 minutes

TOTAL TIME
1 hour
15 minutes

SERVES
4

**TOOLS /
EQUIPMENT**

Zester

Citrus reamer

2 large bowls

Ceramic or glass
baking dish

Baking sheet

Wire cooling rack

⅔ cup rolled oats

⅓ cup packed brown sugar, plus
3 tablespoons for fruit

¼ cup plus 2 tablespoons all-purpose
flour, divided

½ teaspoon ground cinnamon

2 teaspoons fresh ginger, finely grated

Kosher salt

¾ stick butter, freezer-cold and cubed

2 pounds peaches or nectarines,
cut into thin wedges

2 cups blueberries

2 teaspoons freshly squeezed
lemon juice

1 teaspoon lemon zest

Mix the dry ingredients.

In a large bowl, stir with a fork to combine the oats,
⅓ cup of brown sugar, ¼ cup plus 1 tablespoon of
flour, and the cinnamon. Add the ginger, a pinch of
salt, and the butter to the mixture, and work the
butter into the dry ingredients with your fingers
until pea-size crumbs remain. Refrigerate.

Preheat the oven to 375°F.

Mix the fruit.

In another large bowl, stir together the peaches
and blueberries with the lemon juice and zest,
the remaining 3 tablespoons of brown sugar, the
remaining tablespoon of flour, and a pinch of
salt. Toss all to combine.

Bake the crisp.

Pour the fruit mixture into a baking dish, then
spoon the oat mixture on top to coat. On a baking
sheet, bake the crisp until the topping is golden
and the juices bubble, 30 to 45 minutes. Allow
the crisp to cool on a wire cooling rack for at least
20 minutes.

Serve.

The crisp is delicious served warm, room temp,
or even cold. It's so virtuous you could even eat
it for breakfast! This fruity number is excellent
all by itself, but it would be amazing topped with
ice cream.

chocolate-pomegranate brownies

PREP TIME
10 minutes

COOK TIME
30 minutes

TOTAL TIME
50 minutes

MAKES

12

TOOLS / EQUIPMENT

Double boiler (see page 39)

Rubber spatula

Parchment paper

Baking dish

Large bowl

Electric mixer

Skewer or toothpick

Wire cooling rack

12 ounces semisweet dark chocolate (such as Callebaut), chopped, divided

1½ sticks butter, cut into cubes

4 eggs

1¼ cup light brown sugar

1 cup all-purpose flour

Seeds from ½ fresh pomegranate, for topping

Preheat the oven to 350°F.

Melt the chocolate.
Using a double boiler, melt half the chocolate and all the butter. Be careful that the water doesn't bubble up into the top saucepan as you do so, or it will ruin the chocolate. Remove the melted chocolate pan from the hot water bath, wipe the base with a dry dish towel to ensure no drips, stir the butter-chocolate mixture together, and set aside.

Prep the baking dish.
Line a square or small rectangular baking dish with parchment long enough that the paper extends beyond edges by at least 2 inches on all sides.

Mix the remaining ingredients.
In a large bowl, use a fork or hand mixer to thoroughly combine the eggs, sugar, and flour. Add the slightly cooled, melted chocolate mixture and the remaining portion of chopped chocolate, stirring to combine.

Bake the brownies.
Pour the mixture into the prepared baking dish, and bake for 25 minutes, or until a skewer or toothpick comes out almost clean. If you jiggle the tin, the center should move just a little. ❯❯

TRY INSTEAD If you cannot find a fresh pomegranate, top the brownies with fresh raspberries. They're just as delicious!

Let the brownies rest.

Cool the brownies on a wire cooling rack for 10 minutes in the pan; then, using the parchment tabs on either side, lift the brownies out.

Serve.

Cut the brownies into squares, and scatter the pomegranate seeds on top. Enjoy the delicious combo of still-molten chocolate and tart, juicy pomegranate!

coconut ice pops

PREP TIME
10 minutes
plus 4 hours to
freeze

COOK TIME
none

SERVES

4–8

**DEPENDING
ON ICE POP
MOLD SIZE**

**TOOLS /
EQUIPMENT**

Zester

Food processor
or blender

Rubber spatula

Ice pop molds or
small paper cups

Wooden ice-
pop sticks

Bobby pins

3 (5.4 ounce) cans unsweetened organic
coconut cream

Juice and finely grated zest of 1 lime

⅓ cup maple syrup or honey

Blend the ingredients.
In a food processor, purée the coconut cream, lime
zest and juice, and maple syrup.

Prep the ice pops.
Pour the puréed mixture into molds or small paper
cups. Insert wooden ice-pop sticks, clipping bobby
pins to the sticks and setting them across the mold
to anchor the sticks in place.

Let the ice pops set.
Freeze the pops for at least 4 hours.

Serve.
To unmold, if using paper cups, simply peel the
paper away and eat. If using ice pop molds, run
briefly under warm water to loosen.

> TRY INSTEAD Swap seeds from a vanilla
> bean for the lime zest. If you add diced
> fresh young coconut, it will be a real treat!

very berry trifle

PREP TIME
20 minutes
plus 1 hour
to chill

COOK TIME
none

SERVES
4

**TOOLS /
EQUIPMENT**

Citrus reamer

Medium bowl

Large bowl

Whisk or
electric mixer

Rubber spatula

4 glasses

Plastic wrap

3 cups mixed berries of your choice

5 tablespoons cane sugar, divided

Juice of 1 lemon

Juice of ½ orange

1 cup mascarpone

2 cups heavy whipping cream

¼ teaspoon pure vanilla extract

Pinch kosher salt

8 ounces sponge, pound cake, or
ladyfingers, sectioned into ½-inch
slices to fit into glasses

Soak the berries.

In a medium bowl, soak the berries in half the sugar
and the lemon and orange juices. Let the mixture
soften for 10 minutes as you prep the cream.

Make the whipped cream.

In a large bowl, whisk together the mascarpone,
heavy cream, vanilla extract, the remaining
2½ tablespoons of sugar, and the salt until soft
peaks form. You can speed the process up by
using a mixer here, but doing it by hand should
take only a few minutes, thanks to the rich body
of the mascarpone.

Assemble the trifle.

In 4 short cylindrical or wide-mouth glasses, arrange
the ladyfingers or cake pieces to cover the bottom.
Spoon the berry mixture onto the cake in an even
layer. Use a rubber spatula to spread the whipped
cream layer on top of the fruit, holding the glass
and turning it in your hand as you spread the cream.
Repeat layering each glass: cake, berry mixture,
and cream, a couple times until the glasses are very
full, ending with the cream on top. Chill, covered in
plastic wrap, for 1 to 3 hours.

Serve.

Serve chilled with spoons long enough to reach to
the bottom of all the layers, and enjoy. Yum!

banana "ice cream"

PREP TIME
7 minutes, plus
1 hour to freeze

COOK TIME
none

SERVES
4

**TOOLS /
EQUIPMENT**

Baking sheet
Food processor
Rubber spatula

1 bunch (5–8) ripe but firm bananas

Pinch kosher salt

delicious additions

Berries
Greek yogurt or crème fraîche
Ground cinnamon
Nut butters
Chocolate

Prep the bananas.

Peel the bananas, and cut them into chunky coins. Freeze for 1 to 2 hours (or overnight) on a baking sheet.

Blend the bananas.

Using a food processor, blend the bananas with just a pinch of salt until they become smooth and creamy, about 5 minutes. Stop periodically and scrape down the bowl. Watch the bananas transform, like magic, into ice cream! If you'd like to add in other flavors, do so now, and pulse again to combine.

Serve.

For best flavor, remove it from the freezer 10 minutes before serving. Cover and freeze any leftovers. Ice cream can be made 5 days ahead.

HELPFUL HINT If your freezer can't accommodate a baking sheet, a metal pie tin or baking dish works in a pinch.

strawberry-rhubarb mini tarts

PREP TIME
30 minutes
plus 1 hour
to chill

COOK TIME
45 minutes

MAKES

8

MINI TARTS

**TOOLS /
EQUIPMENT**

Zester

Food processor

Plastic wrap

Large bowl

Rolling pin

2 baking sheets

Parchment paper

Pastry brush

Wire cooling rack

FOR THE DOUGH

2½ cups all-purpose flour

1 teaspoon cane sugar, plus 1 teaspoon
for sprinkling

1 teaspoon kosher salt

2 sticks butter, freezer-cold and
chopped into small cubes

¼ cup ice water

FOR THE FILLING

¾ pound rhubarb, rinsed, ends trimmed,
cut into ¼-inch pieces

2 pints fresh strawberries, rinsed and
hulled, cut into ¼-inch pieces

½ cup cane sugar

Zest of 1 orange

¼ cup orange juice

Pinch kosher salt

Make the dough.

In a food processor, pulse the flour, sugar, and salt to
combine. Add the cold butter and pulse 5 to 7 times,
until the butter mixes with the flour to form pea-size
crumbs. In a slow stream, add the ice water while
pulsing, stopping once the dough holds together.

Test the dough.

To test, unplug the food processor, open the lid, and
press some dough together. If it holds together, it's
ready. If it still crumbles, add a bit more ice water
as you pulse a few more times. You may use slightly
less or slightly more than ¼ cup of water.

Place the dough on a long sheet of plastic wrap.

Separate the dough into two mounds, then flatten
each to form a disk. Cut the plastic wrap in two
between the disks, and wrap each. Refrigerate for
at least 20 minutes to let it firm up.

Make the filling.

In a large bowl, carefully mix together the rhubarb,
strawberries, sugar, orange zest, orange juice, and
salt. Cover with plastic wrap, and let the flavors meld,
at least 15 minutes.

Roll the dough.

On a lightly floured surface, cut each disk into four.
Chill the rest as you roll each one out. Roll from the
center to the edge, turning an eighth turn with each
pass of the rolling pin, until the dough is ⅛ inch thick.
(They don't have to be perfect circles. Patch any
large tears with dough pinched from the edge.) »

PRO TIPS:

- For the best results, cube cold butter and then place in a container in the freezer for 20 minutes. w
- For even baking, crimp a strip of foil over any parts that you don't want to brown further.
- You can make the dough ahead and keep it wrapped, refrigerated, for a few days, or it can be wrapped tightly and frozen for up to 3 weeks. To thaw, refrigerate overnight.
- The fruit mixture can also be made in advance and in fact benefits from a day or two of melding in the refrigerator.
- Cook any leftover fruit over low heat to make compote for yogurt, ice cream, muffins, or toast.

Assemble the tarts.
Line two baking sheets with parchment paper, and lay the rolled pastry 2 to 3 inches apart from each other. Spoon mounds of the fruit mixture into the center of each pastry, dividing the filling evenly and leaving a 1-inch border around the edge. Assemble one set of tarts at a time, leaving the other batch of pastry in the refrigerator.

Crimp the tart edges.
Gather the pastry edges, making pleats onto the piled fruit. Lightly brush water in between the folds to press the pastry together and keep it in place. If the dough becomes flabby, it needs to be rechilled.

Refrigerate the tarts.
Once you have filled and crimped the tarts, refrigerate them for at least 1 hour before baking.

Repeat steps 5 through 8 with the remaining dough.

Preheat the oven to 400°F.

Bake the tarts.
Very lightly brush the edges of the pastry with water, and sprinkle with the reserved 1 teaspoon of sugar. Bake for 30 minutes, or until the crusts are golden, then lower the temperature to 375°F and bake for 10 to 15 minutes, until the juices bubble and the crust is deeply golden. Transfer the tarts to a wire cooling rack to cool.

Serve.
Remove the tarts when they can be easily handled, and enjoy them warm. Store leftover tarts at room temperature, wrapped loosely in foil, for 2 days.

chocolate-cherry bark

PREP TIME
10 minutes
plus 15 minutes
to chill

COOK TIME
10 minutes

MAKES

1

SHEET

**TOOLS /
EQUIPMENT**

Double boiler
(see page 39)

Parchment paper

Baking sheet

Rubber spatula

1 pound bittersweet dark chocolate,
cut into small pieces

2 cups granola of your choice

1 cup dried sour cherries,
coarsely chopped

Flake salt, such as Maldon

Prep the chocolate and the sheet pan.
In a double boiler, melt the chocolate. Place parchment paper on a baking sheet, and pour the granola into a pile on it.

Mix the bark together.
Once the chocolate is molten, pour it onto the granola, and using a rubber spatula, mix the two together thoroughly. As you mix, spread the chocolate-covered granola into an even layer on the baking sheet. Keep spreading until the mixture reaches the edges, ending up about ¼ inch thick.

Add the sweet and salty accents.
Scatter the chopped cherries around, pressing them lightly into the bark, and then scatter on the salt. Use the salt as an accent more than a ground cover.

Let the bark set.
Place the baking sheet in a cool place to harden. Refrigerate for 15 minutes if you prefer to accelerate its cooling. Break the mixture into pieces. Refrigerate in a sealed container to store.

Serve.
Remove the bark from the refrigerator half an hour before serving to allow the flavors to fully bloom. Serve on a platter. It keeps for 2 weeks, refrigerated—if it lasts that long!

 HELPFUL HINT This delectable bark can be prepared 2 days in advance.

SETTING THE TABLE

The best part of preparing a meal is sharing it with family and friends: a little thoughtfulness on arranging the table and seating guests is worthwhile. A few simple guidelines will help you create a warm and welcoming feeling, whether for a casual lunch or a holiday feast.

Basic Table Setting A basic table is set with a knife, fork, and spoon framing the dinner plate. They are set out in the order of use: fork to the left of plate, knife to the right, and a soup- or dessertspoon to the right of the knife. A napkin can be rolled or folded and laid on the plate.

Glasses Each place setting should have all of the glasses needed for the meal. Water glasses sit on the right of each plate, just above the knife. For a meal with wine for grown-ups, place the wine glass above and to the left of the water glass.

Dishes On a daily basis, all you'll need is a single plate or large shallow bowl (for pasta, soup, or stew). For a more formal meal with many courses, add a bread plate to the left side of the setting, and a salad plate or soup bowl on top of the napkin and dinner plate, making an impressive display all guests will notice.

Silverware No matter how formal or casual your meal, set the silverware in the order of use, from the outside in. For multiple courses,

the fork for the first course (like salad) is the farthest to the left, followed by another fork for the main course. To the right of the plate, place a knife and if you need a soupspoon, place it on the far right. Lay dessert silverware horizontally above the plate, but for a casual meal, simply bring the silverware in with dessert.

Mix-and-Match Choosing plates and glasses from the same dish set automatically creates a harmonious table, but using different kinds of dishes, silverware, and glasses can be equally beautiful. An eclectic setting is more creative and lets your imagination guide the display. If you choose a mix-and-match theme, have one element tie everything together, such as the same napkin, the same scale for each plate, or a similar color scheme.

Extras There are infinite ways to make a table setting special. For example, an apple or leaf on top of each napkin, or a small vase with flowers transforms a regular meal into a special one. Place cards can make the table feel more formal. The twinkle of candles also makes for a great experience.

So, leave enough time during your food preparation to put these finishing touches in place. Then you can proudly watch your guests enjoy the fruits of your hard work, making the experience all the sweeter.

Appendix B
CONVERSION CHARTS

Volume Equivalents (Liquid)

US STANDARD	US STANDARD (OUNCES)	METRIC (APPROXIMATE)
2 tablespoons	1 fl. oz.	30 mL
¼ cup	2 fl. oz.	60 mL
½ cup	4 fl. oz.	120 mL
1 cup	8 fl. oz.	240 mL
1½ cups	12 fl. oz.	355 mL
2 cups or 1 pint	16 fl. oz.	475 mL
4 cups or 1 quart	32 fl. oz.	1 L
1 gallon	128 fl. oz.	4 L

Oven Temperatures

FAHRENHEIT (F)	CELSIUS (C) (APPROXIMATE)
250°F	120°C
300°F	150°C
325°F	165°C
350°F	180°C
375°F	190°C
400°F	200°C
425°F	220°C
450°F	230°C

Volume Equivalents (Dry)

US STANDARD	METRIC (APPROXIMATE)
⅛ teaspoon	0.5 mL
¼ teaspoon	1 mL
½ teaspoon	2 mL
¾ teaspoon	4 mL
1 teaspoon	5 mL
1 tablespoon	15 mL
¼ cup	59 mL
⅓ cup	79 mL
½ cup	118 mL
⅔ cup	156 mL
¾ cup	177 mL
1 cup	235 mL
2 cups or 1 pint	475 mL
3 cups	700 mL
4 cups or 1 quart	1 L

Weight Equivalents

US STANDARD	METRIC (APPROXIMATE)
½ ounce	15 g
1 ounce	30 g
2 ounces	60 g
4 ounces	115 g
8 ounces	225 g
12 ounces	340 g
16 ounces or 1 pound	455 g

GLOSSARY

Al dente This Italian term describes a food, usually pasta, when it is done but still firm—literally, "to the teeth."

Arugula Arugula is a dark green salad leaf with a mustardy, peppery flavor.

Basil Basil is a highly fragrant plant that is part of the mint family with more than 60 varieties. Whenever possible, choose fresh basil over the dried form. Basil leaves should look vibrant and free from darks spots or dried edges. It should be stored in the refrigerator wrapped between layers of slightly damp paper towels, sealed in a container or bag.

Bay leaf Bay leaves are aromatic laurel leaves and are used to flavor soups and stews. They do not soften when cooked and should not be eaten. Remove it when you find one. They keep dried for 6 months in a cool, dark place.

Blanch To blanch means to plunge food into boiling water for a brief amount of time. Most blanched foods are immediately transferred to an ice bath to stop the cooking process, also known as "shocking." Blanching raw vegetables brightens their color while maintaining a tender, crisp, barely cooked texture and flavor. Blanching also helps loosen the skin of tomatoes or stone fruit for peeling.

Bonito flakes Bonito is a kind of tuna, and bonito flakes (*katsuobushi* in Japanese, where the flakes originate) are the wispy shavings of dried and smoked bonito. Bonito flakes have a very savory, somewhat smoky taste, and are a great accent for all kinds of foods when you want to deepen the overall flavor.

Caramelize To caramelize is to cook something until it forms a deeply golden crust and the inherent sugars break down, intensifying a food's sweetness. For instance, caramelizing onions replaces their sharp flavor with a savory sweetness.

Cayenne pepper Hot and pungent cayenne pepper is one of the most widely used spicy ingredients. Avoid touching your eyes or other sensitive body parts after you've touched cayenne pepper, and wash your hands thoroughly with warm soapy water when you are finished. Dry peppers or cayenne powder can be stored at room temperature in a cool, dark place in an airtight container for several months.

Chile peppers Chile peppers are small peppers that make food spicy. Capsaicin is the chemical substance that makes chile peppers hot and the white membranes that hold the seeds contain the most. It highly irritates the skin and eyes, so always wash your hands immediately after cutting a chile.

Chili powder Chili powder is a spice blend for making chili that contains oregano, cumin, and garlic as well as dried hot chiles.

Chives Chives are part of the allium family. They impart a pleasantly subtle, onion-garlic flavor to savory foods. Chives are high in fiber, antioxidants, and vitamin K, which strengthens bones and maintains brain health. Chive stalks are hollow and quite slender, and look like lush bunches of foot-high grass. Their lavender blossoms are also edible.

Cilantro Cilantro has very green, papery, and tender leaves, and should be eaten fresh (the stems are edible, too). Season cooked foods at the last moment so the cilantro doesn't wilt. To store fresh cilantro, place them in a jar with water and cover with a plastic bag, and place in the refrigerator. Depending on its treatment at the market, cilantro should last up to a week in the refrigerator. Do not wash cilantro until you need it, since excess moisture can make the leaves slimy during storage.

Cinnamon Cinnamon is a fragrant, sweet-flavored spice used since biblical times for its medicinal and culinary benefits. It is the inner bark of a tropical evergreen tree, which curls into sticks when dried. Cinnamon is known to have antioxidant, antidiabetic, antiseptic, anti-inflammatory, and anti-flatulent properties.

Compost Compost is decomposed organic matter, a natural process of recycling organic material such as leaves and vegetable scraps. When you compost organic waste, nutrients are returned to the soil, nourishing everything that grows out of it.

Coriander Coriander is the dried round seed from the cilantro plant and has a spicy, citrus flavor. The seeds are often used toasted whole, which brings out their aromatic quality and essential oils, and then ground.

Cumin Cumin is a seed with a nutty, peppery flavor. It is an excellent source of iron, which helps keep the immune system healthy. It is a great seasoning for lentils, rice, chickpeas, and black beans, or as part of a spice mixture to roast meats, as well as boosting the flavors of salsas and sauces.

Dill Dill has green, wispy, fernlike leaves and imparts a tangy, sweet taste. Whenever possible, choose fresh dill over dried, which has little flavor. Dill stalks droop soon after being picked. Store fresh dill in the refrigerator, wrapped in layers of damp paper towel and then sealed in a container, or in a jar of water with a bag placed over the leaves. Since dill is very fragile, it will keep for only 3 to 4 days.

Divided Seen in ingredient lists, this term means that you won't use all of that ingredient at once. The instructions tell you how much to use and when.

Emulsify Emulsify means to combine two liquids together that do not ordinarily mix easily. The ingredients are usually oil or other type of fat and another liquid like water or broth. By constantly whisking these two different liquids together, the result is a thick, creamy liquid with a silky texture. Some familiar emulsions include hollandaise, mayonnaise or aioli, salad dressing, and crème anglaise.

English cucumber English cucumbers, also known as hothouse, greenhouse, or seedless cucumbers, are long and thin and have a milder, sweeter flavor. Its skin is thinner, and it contains smaller, less noticeable seeds. They are sold wrapped in plastic sleeves in the produce sections in grocery stores.

Flake salt Flake salt consists of sheer, lacy pyramid-like crystals, with a bright, clean, sparkly flavor. It is great on salads, fresh vegetables, roasted seafood, and fish. This salt dissolves quickly and should be added just before serving.

Ginger Ginger is an aromatic, pungent and spicy rhizome (root), prized for its medicinal and culinary properties. Fresh ginger has the best flavor and health benefits, and lasts up to 3 weeks unpeeled in the refrigerator. When purchasing fresh ginger, make sure the root is firm, smooth, and blemish free. If it is very young, it won't need peeling. Otherwise, the brown, papery skin on mature ginger root should be scraped off with a spoon.

GMO *GMO* stands for "genetically modified organism." It is produced by a laboratory process that uses genes from the DNA of one species and artificially combines them with the genes of another species of plant or animal. These genes may come from bacteria, viruses, insects, animals, or even humans. This process is often referred to as genetic engineering (GE) and operates in ways that are not possible or desirable in nature. This technique has not been lab-tested in a conclusive way before being planted in the field and leads to unpredictable changes in the DNA.

Gruyère Gruyere cheese is a traditional, unpasteurized, semi-hard cheese. It is an excellent melting cheese, used prominently in gratins, croques monsieurs and mesdames, and for grilled cheese, omelettes, and mac 'n' cheese.

Haloumi Haloumi cheese is a brined, slightly springy white cheese, traditionally made from sheep and goat milk. Its texture is similar to mozzarella or a firm feta. Haloumi can be easily fried or grilled, and is often served with watermelon and mint, or as part of *meze*, a Mediterranean appetizer platter of various savory foods.

Harissa Harissa is a spicy, aromatic chile paste widely used in North African and Middle Eastern cooking. It comes in tubes, jars, or cans, or you can choose a powdered spice version. Harissa is sold in Middle Eastern markets or in the specialty section of grocery stores.

Kosher salt Kosher salt has flaky white grains that dissolve slowly in cooking. Chefs favor it because its large grains make it easier to pinch between fingers, offering a tighter control on seasoning and because it also lacks the additives found in table salt, like iodine. Use kosher salt for general cooking, including recipes that specify coarse salt.

Labneh Labneh is a tangy, creamy Lebanese cheese made from strained yogurt. Custard-like in its consistency, it can be used in savory or sweet dishes. Look for labneh in Middle Eastern and specialty markets.

Meyer lemon Meyer lemons are sweeter in flavor than other lemons and have a floral aroma. Choose lemons that are deeply yellow, plump, and fragrant when you gently rub the skin.

Mint Mint is a hardy herb with vibrant green leaves and a fresh, sweet flavor with a cool aftertaste. There are more than 20 varieties, the most common being peppermint and spearmint. Use a sharp knife and slice mint leaves gently, as overchopping will bruise them. Store fresh mint in the refrigerator, carefully wrapped in damp paper towel and inside a loosely closed plastic bag. It should keep fresh for several days.

Mirin Mirin is a light golden wine that is a staple of Japanese cooking, lending its sweet flavor to contrast with other Asian sauces, such as soy sauce. Mirin is extremely versatile and a little goes a long way. Look for it in Asian markets or in the specialty section of the grocery store.

Miso Miso is fermented soybeans and is central to Japanese cooking. Usually a thick paste, its consistency is similar to peanut butter. Dark miso has a stronger, more pungent flavor, which enhances beef or lamb dishes. Light-colored miso is more delicate and used for soup, salad dressings, and sauces. Miso is one of the few nonmeat foods that contains all essential amino acids, which makes it a complete protein. It should be stored in the refrigerator in a tightly sealed container, and it keeps for up to one year.

Mustard seed Mustard seeds are the fruit pods from the mustard plant. There are many varieties of mustard plants, but the principal ones are black, white, and brown mustard. Black mustard seeds have a strong, pungent taste, while white mustard seeds (which are actually a soft yellow color) are milder.

Nutmeg Nutmeg is the inner kernel of a fruit from a tropical evergreen plant. Whole nutmeg grates easily and gives the best spicy flavor, and keeps indefinitely.

Oregano Oregano is a shrub with green oval leaves and white or pink edible flowers. It imparts a warm, peppery, and somewhat bitter flavor to foods. Whenever possible, choose fresh oregano over dried. Fresh oregano should be stored in the refrigerator wrapped in damp paper towel and sealed in a container.

Organic Certified organic foods are foods produced by farming methods that are free of synthetic additives like pesticides and chemical fertilizers and were not processed through genetic engineering, ionizing radiation, or industrial solvents. Eating organically grown food is a great way to limit exposure to cancer-causing contaminants and toxic heavy metals that are commonly found in foods grown using conventional agricultural practices. In addition to reducing exposure to these harmful substances, supporting growers of organically grown foods often means supporting local and small family farms.

Oxidation Oxidation occurs when foods are exposed to oxygen. When a food is peeled, sliced, diced, cut, mashed, or shredded, a reaction between their enzymes and oxygen in the air causes the food to turn brown. Apples, bananas, and avocados show oxidation whenever they are cut or peeled.

Paprika Paprika is made from ground bonnet pepper, a relative of chile peppers and bell peppers. It can be sweet, hot, or smoky. Fresh paprika has a lot of flavor, but it diminishes quickly as it ages.

Parsley The two most widely available types of parsley are curly and the broader Italian flat-leaf parsley. Italian parsley is more fragrant and holds up better in cooking. Choose fresh parsley that is deep green in color and looks crisp. Fresh parsley should be washed just before using and should be added toward the end of the cooking process to retain its taste, color, and nutritional value.

Persian cucumber Persian cucumbers have smooth, thin skin, and their flesh is very crisp and sweet. They have no developed seeds, and measure 4 to 6 inches in length. They can be used interchangeably with English or kirby cucumbers.

Quartered Seen in ingredient lists and instructions, this means to cut the ingredient into four pieces of roughly equal size.

Red pepper flakes Red pepper flakes and crushed red pepper are pulverized, dried red chile peppers, and impart a somewhat sharp, smoky flavor to foods.

Reduce This term is often used in reference to liquids. It means to cook down so that the liquid amount decreases. To "reduce by half" means to cook until you have half as much liquid as you started with, which concentrates flavor as the volume evaporates.

Rosemary Rosemary is an evergreen shrub with hardy quills that resemble flat pine needles. Most recipes call for the quills, or leaves, but you can also add a whole sprig to season a dish and remove it before serving. Quickly rinse rosemary under cool running water and pat dry before adding it to dishes.

Roux A flour-and-fat (usually butter) mixture used to thicken soups and sauces.

Sumac Sumac is a spice with a lemony flavor. It is used in dry rubs for lamb, chicken, and fish, marinades for meat or vegetable shish kabobs and sprinkled onto salads and dips.

Thyme Thyme is a fragrant herb with thin, woody stems and small, pungent leaves. You can add fresh thyme by adding whole sprigs or stripping leaves from the stems.

Trivet A trivet is an object placed beneath a hot serving dish, skillet, or roasting pan to protect a surface from heat or moisture damage. Trivets are made from metal, ceramic, wood, cork, or fabric such as felt.

Za'atar Za'atar is Arabic for "thyme." It is a Middle Eastern spice blend using thyme as well as toasted sesame seeds, sumac, and sea salt. Za'atar is used to add earthy savoriness to hearty soups and as a rub for chicken and lamb. A light sprinkling also enhances eggs, tomatoes, and feta cheese.

RECIPE INDEX

INDEX

....

ACKNOWLEDGMENTS

To Ma and Pa and Guiseppe, I love you so. Thank you for unconditionally loving me and believing in my creative spirit, and for your thoughtful feedback as I made this book. I am grateful to be part of such a wonderful family.

To Jim, my sweetheart and life partner, thank you for enthusiastically eating all my bright ideas and for compassionately sharing feedback and shaping who I've become. Happily, those bright ideas have gotten pretty good by now.

To Mark Tulloss, in that rickety apartment back in the early days in West Philadelphia, you sparked my interest in what delicious food could be.

To my editor Meg, you saw the potential of fantastic new work we could make together. I am so grateful you thought I should be the person to breathe life into this great book, and for our continued relationship.

To Katy, Maggie, Wendy, and the whole Callisto team, your vision and critical thinking have been a blessing. Thank you for working with me, brilliantly piecing together a written work for kids. And thanks for including children in the landscape of delicious, healthy cooking, aiding in their delicious futures.

Thank you for your generosity and support: Bryant Terry, Susan Spungen, Betty Fussell, Phyllis Grant, Aran Goyoaga, Jon Rowley, Graymarket Textile Design, Sorella Le Var, dear Instagram friends, and GIR silicone kitchen gear. Your support has fueled me on a continuous basis, often giving an extra boost to my day.

Thank you small family farmers, for producing the most beautiful produce, eggs, and meat for me to cook, style, photograph, and then, hungrily eat. Your tireless work makes the difference for more and more of us in the contemporary food landscape.

Big thanks to my kid chef recipe testers, Miles (10), Olivia (10), and Lili (7), who made my recipes at home and offered helpful suggestions for improvements. You helped make my recipes even clearer!